Lyalya UMIRZAKOVA

# STALIN'S BLOODY REIGN 1924-1953

2022

# CONTENTS

## COPYRIGHT

This book edition first published in 2022 (print and electronic)



Cover design by Lyalya Umirzakova
Translated by Teresa Pearce



ISBN 978-617-7836-15-4

## PREFACE

This book is about the Kazakhs, my own people. I love them dearly and am proud to number myself among them, and I care deeply about their fate and that of my country.

I have set out to share with you, dear reader, my thoughts concerning Stalin, the man who condemned Kazakhs, Ukrainians, Germans, Koreans, Jews and other ethnic groups to horrific suffering and visited a monstrous and bloody tragedy on the Kazakhs. The book rests on a reliable and authoritative source – my father and father-in-law's eyewitness accounts of what they saw, heard and experienced during their lifetimes. It has obviously not been possible to describe everything in full. The subject I have chosen is wide-ranging and highly sensitive, involving information that remains classified. I have summoned up the courage to write about the Holodomor, the famine that was artificially engineered by Stalin in the 20th century – a famine unprecedented in human history. My own views are closely interwoven through the writing, and I express my feelings about the narratives I have heard. Perhaps for that reason, these harrowing reminiscences that have been preserved for so many years are presented as freeform notes following no strict system.


Lyalya Umirzakova
2022

**PART ONE**

We need to know our country's history. That history is made up of the stories of all the families living in this country. Each family is a tiny part of this vast nation. Our ancestors struggled for freedom and independence. We must treasure our ancestors' heritage, including the history of our clan, and treasure the blessed memory of family members and loved ones who went before us. Their actions, life experience, extraordinary courage and patriotism serve as an example for their descendants to follow.

Memories are without price. It is not always possible to keep mementos and photographs. But the stories told of real-life historical events must be handed down from generation to generation and replenished with new ones. This book is an attempt to preserve memories – that thread that links the generations – so that the memory is not forgotten, erased or lost, but lives on for as long as our clan exists.

I truly believe that in this way, grain by grain, it will be possible to piece together a history of the Kazakh people.

1.

As soon as my husband and I graduated and received our degrees, we went with our little daughter to live with my husband's parents. My in-laws were respectable, honourable people with big hearts, wide-open souls, and a unique ability to create an atmosphere of warmth. We were wrapped in such an all-encompassing love that we didn't notice how quickly time was slipping past. A fascinating new chapter in my life had begun in which I was constantly surrounded by people who had become immeasurably dear, beloved and close to me. Each day was lit up with a special light and brought new joys, excitements and enjoyable jobs to do.

My second father, my father-in-law Temirbolat Tynybekuly, was highborn, a member of the nobility. His father, Tynybek Omirzakuly, a *bolys*[1], lived in the Ayaguz district in East Kazakhstan, 70 km from the regional capital. Tynybek Ata's[2] land stretched from Lake Balkhash to the Tarbagatai mountains, an area populated by over 300 Kazakhs. He also owned more than two thousand horses, which were taken out to pasture by herdsmen. They wintered near Lake Balkhash; the spring and autumn pastures were situated in the valleys by Lake Alakol, and the summer *jailyau*[3] was in the Tarbagatai mountains.

In those days there was a village (now a town) named Karsakpai, about 100 km from the present-day city of Zhezkazgan. According to the elders, during the period of peace, some Englishmen turned up prospecting for minerals. On discovering copper ore in the village, they built a copper smelter, where they also smelted gold and silver. A large processing business was built up and ore mining developed rapidly. When the land around present-day Zhezkazgan was surveyed, further copper deposits were discovered. A branch railway line was laid down to transport the ore from there to Karsakpai. Throughout the region, for about 100 km in every direction, living standards improved as people now had money for food and other necessities.

Once they were settled, the English expanded their business. Copper ore was also found in the area where the city of Balkhash is now. To transport it to Karsakpai, it was planned to build a railway linking Balkhash and Zhezkazgan.

The English approached Tynybek Ata to conduct negotiations with regard to the mining of copper ore from his lands. The copper ore deposits in the area around Lake Balkhash (now the town of Sayak) provided an incentive for them to work together. The English drew up a contract with Tynybek Ata, and they began to collaborate on the copper ore mining project.

It was Tynybek Ata who had the idea of building a general hospital in Ayaguz, the principal city of the district, as well as

---

[1] *bolys* – a Kazakh nobleman
[2] *ata* - grandfather
[3] *jailyau* – summer pastures in highland meadows

schools and homes for the workers. He put forward the suggestion and financed the purchase of the necessary building materials. He recruited doctors and arranged for young women to travel to Omsk to do six-month nursing training courses. It was in this hospital that my father-in-law was born.

In peacetime, Tynybek Ata sold horses to Tsar Nicholas II's army. During the First World War he supplied the Russian army with horses free of charge. Surprisingly, there was corruption even then: records show that only 30-40% of the two hundred horses got through. But Tynybek Ata was glad anyway. His gifts did not go unnoticed by Nicholas II, who awarded him a signed certificate of commendation and a seven-shot revolver, sent by courier, as a mark of his gratitude. In addition to the award, the tsar exempted men from Tynybek Ata's *aul*[4] from being called up for field work.

**Explanatory note:** Muslims were not conscripted during the First World War; they were deployed only in the Labour Army. I believe the reason why Kazakhs were excluded from fighting in the war was due to the Russians' reluctance to train them.

The period following the First World War was a time of unrest and upheaval. Kazakhstan felt the weight of the powerful nationalist yoke of the Russian Empire as the expropriation of fertile Kazakh land continued. Migrants settled on the seized land.

In October 1917 the red revolution began. The Bolsheviks came to the people with slogans like "Peace to all peoples!", "All power to the Soviets!", "Land for the peasants!", "Factories for the workers!", "Bread for the hungry!" The people believed them, supported them and helped bring them to power. They did not know that the slogans were merely a smokescreen behind which lurked only lies. The Bolsheviks were led by Lenin. It was he who "promoted his 'junior' fellow-soldier" Joseph Stalin, appointing him People's Commissar for Nationalities at the end of 1917 and General Secretary of the Central Committee

---

[4] *aul* – Kazakh village

of the Russian Communist Party (Bolsheviks) in April 1922. "Now no one could prevent Stalin from becoming the 'leader of all times and peoples' in the near future."

Stalin couldn't have cared less about all those slogans – ordinary people's problems were of no concern to him.

The Bolsheviks seized power. They were atheists who did not acknowledge or believe in God or religion of any kind. Their only idols were the Communists. They stirred up the masses and fanned the flames of conflict. They operated on the principle that anything touched by the hand of the bourgeoisie was to be purged and eliminated.

Concerned by these developments, the English took the decision to leave in 1918. Tynybek was offered the chance to go too, but he declared that he would never leave his ancestral home. The English never managed to complete the railway line between Balkhash and Zhezkazgan. And all that remains today is a chimney, the ruins of the smelting plant, the railway embankment from Karsakpai to Zhezkazgan, and the bridges over the river Sarysu – silent witnesses of the area's former inhabitants.

Tynybek Ata was harassed by the Red Guard for having helped the Russian tsar. He said to the villagers, "The red revolutionaries are hounding me. You too may suffer because of me, so gather together your families and your animals and go." But they did not do as he said, answering, "Tynybek, we have lived through good times together with you, and together with you we will get through the hard times. We will stay with you come what may."

In 1920 some prosperous Russians from the *aul* who were getting ready to leave for China invited Tynybek Ata to go with them. But he was resolute: "Here I was born, and here I shall die."

It wasn't long before the Reds appeared in Ayaguz, sweeping down unexpectedly like a destructive and deadly whirlwind. They set fire to the hospital, the Orthodox church and the mosque, demolished hotels, smashed up inns, and pulled down shops and all the other buildings.

In the summer of 1929, the marauders reached the *aul* of Tynybek Ata. They annihilated the *aul* totally, slaughtering over 220 people, leaving not one soul alive. They felt no pity for newborn babies, pregnant women, or grey-haired old men. They set fire to houses and crops and shot at women as they ran from their burning homes with no time to collect any belongings. Within minutes, there was nothing left of the *aul* but a heap of burnt-out ruins and charred corpses. Who were these people who were so put out by the peace-loving villagers? A baying pack of rabid, ravenous jackals, mangy, cowardly and rotten to the core, who had sniffed out easy pickings and were eager to please their lion overlords by humbly carrying out their orders, ready to run off to do their bidding. They were prepared to destroy everything that fell into their hands for the sake of glory and reward. No one was spared. How is it possible that these stinking, loathsome, screeching, howling creatures ruthlessly slaughtered my kinsfolk? Hearing about these events is so horrific and terrifying that I cannot be calm about it. Who could? My father-in-law Temirbolat, then in his teens, was not in the *aul* when this vicious attack took place. He had gone to the stables to supervise the herdsmen, and his sisters Sania and Balzia were visiting their maternal grandmother. Thus, by a miracle, the brother and sisters escaped with their lives.

When they returned home to find the mutilated bodies of their parents, their elder brother and fellow villagers, bent into unnatural poses, they collapsed in shock. The corpses bore the marks of unspeakable atrocities. They were utterly horror-struck. Hunched over their loved ones' rigid faces, they kissed and stroked them as if their tear-soaked caresses might bring their dear ones back to life. They wiped away the clotted blood, and with trembling fingers they gently smoothed the wrinkles that the savage pain had etched onto their faces. They wept noisily and uncontrollably, drowning in grief and compassion for their parents who had been taken from them for ever. They had not breath or strength enough to scream. They hugged and comforted one another…

It was too dangerous to stay. The marauders might come back for them at any moment. They had to leave urgently. They fled, trying not to attract attention, walking under cover of night. By day they hid in ravines. They huddled close together, hugging and warming each other with their breath. Any suspicious rustling noises frightened them half to death; their knees shook and they clenched their hands so hard that their nails pressed deep into their palms. For five years they wandered, drifting between relatives and friends of their father. At first they had no thought of leaving their homeland. Foreign lands seemed to them alien and unknown. But there was nowhere to hide. This could not go on. Elders advised them to leave the country. The three siblings were forced to cross the Chinese border and ended up in a town named Chauchek. There they remained. They met Alexei and Maria, a married couple they had known in Ayaguz who had helped with the building of the hospital and moved to China in 1920. When Alexei and Maria had decided to leave, they had invited Tynybek Ata's family to come too, but they had flatly refused, saying, "This is our homeland, the land of our forefathers." Once in China, Alexei and Maria had carried on farming, expanding their business and earning a good income. They were delighted to see their fellow villagers and compatriots and offered them building work. Together they built a school, a cultural centre for the town, an outdoor cinema, and a park of culture and recreation. They also became close friends. Little by little, things got better. Despite living in a foreign country, cut off from their homeland, they retained their language, culture, traditions and customs.

After everything she had been through, Maria used to suffer from severe spells of anxiety that at any moment everything might collapse and fall apart.

Gradually the three siblings began to get used to their new life. The sisters got married. Temirbolat did his best to help those less fortunate than himself. He gave shelter and support to homeless young people and got them back on their feet. In 1947 he married.

No one knows how Stalin sniffed out the educated Kazakhs and well-off Russians in China who had been forced to leave the Kazakh Republic, but when he did, he dispatched his henchmen to China. These "masters of the universe" wasted no time in carrying out Stalin's instructions to track down Kazakh refugees and slaughter them in cold blood. Rumours reached Alexei and Maria that these fiends were in Chinese territory. Maria remembered her misgivings. Her darkest fears were justified. Suspecting the worst, they packed up literally overnight and left, travelling deep into China to Harbin. Temirbolat Tynybekuly and his wife, children and sisters did not go with them. The parting was heart-wrenching and tearful. They lay low in a safe place, waiting until Stalin's emissaries should leave.

Temirbolat Tynybekuly mourned desperately for his native land. His soul ached with grief for his dead parents and brother. His former neighbours used to appear before him in visions as if they were alive. His heart was racked with an insatiable yearning. In moments of clarity he longed to take revenge on the Red fanatics for his parents' death. Knowing, however, that there was no prospect of vengeance, he would sink to his knees and clench his teeth and fists from rage and frustration until they ached. He tried to distract himself with work so as not to be driven mad by what he had gone through. Isolated and beside himself with grief, he wept in secret and numbed the pain in his soul. He comforted himself with the faint hope of returning to Kazakhstan, oppressed by the intolerable wait for news.
In April 1962 the border was opened for two or three days for those wishing to return to Kazakhstan. Temirbolat and his wife and children didn't hesitate. They had no time to pack properly. They took the clothes they needed, but their hearts were racing with the joy and excitement of travelling to their homeland, and in their haste, they completely forgot about their documents. Property and bank deposits – a serious amount of savings – were also left behind.
Temirbolat and his family returned to their homeland. But they were not met with open arms. The policy of harassment, a plank of domestic policy at the time, caused them enormous distress. Anyone who had left their native land was considered a sworn enemy and a traitor to their people. They were labelled "Chinese", insulted and humiliated; their children were not accepted at Party schools, and they could not move up the career

ladder. At work they won no awards or honorary titles for their service; even the most distinguished were never selected as conference delegates, and never awarded the title of Hero of Socialist Labour or other honorifics with which other outstanding workers were rewarded.

I have first-hand knowledge of this. My husband was born in China. He was a small boy when he returned with his parents and he never lived in China again. Yet despite having spent his childhood, youth and the rest of his life in his native Kazakhstan, the land of his forefathers, he was stuck with the "Chinese" label for years, although in fairness it must be said that not everyone called him that. I regard anyone who indulged in this sort of name-calling as ignorant and rude. I remember how even some of my own (!) relatives (aunts and uncles), on hearing of my forthcoming marriage, tried to talk me out of it, asking why I was marrying a "Chinaman". I had never got into arguments or conflicts with family members before, but I was bold enough to stand my ground. It was my choice, my love and my life, and I was not about to go back on our decision because of their stupid irrational beliefs. I didn't understand how they could not see the person. I thought their attempts to dissuade me by using an offensive label were pointless and, worse, insensitive.

In those days people used to look askance at returnees. It was the Soviet ideology. They had no idea what their compatriots had been through, what they had experienced. Or perhaps they did know but kept quiet because it was a taboo subject. They were afraid.

Kabdesh Zhumadilov, a well-known Soviet and Kazakhstani writer, was born in China on 25 April 1936, and it was there that he started writing. His early works were published in Chinese newspapers and magazines. When he returned to Kazakhstan, his historic homeland, he continued on his creative and literary journey, worked on national publications, and produced wonderful books that were much loved by Kazakhstani readers. Despite his talent, his place of birth proved to be an obstacle to success, and it was many years before he was admitted to the writers' union. He was awarded the title "People's Writer of Kazakhstan" in 1998.

2.

My father-in-law's cousin Torebai Aǧa[5] remembered how the monsters appeared in their village, sweeping down like vultures, breaking into houses, pillaging and murdering. He was the youngest child. He was five years old. When the marauders broke into their yard, his father and elder brothers were working on the farm. His mother was getting lunch ready. Hearing clattering noises and muffled voices, she looked out of the window. Sensing that something wasn't right, she just had time to snatch up Torebai and hide behind the stove. The murderers had already shot her husband and children. Now they burst into the house. They didn't notice anyone hiding; they didn't search the rooms particularly thoroughly. They must have been in a hurry. Mother and son sat absolutely still for about two hours with not a peep out of the little boy. When they emerged, Torebai's mother rushed outside. There, around the cart, lay the lifeless bodies of her loved ones. They had been shot in the head. Mad with grief, she tore at her hair. The blood froze in her veins. When she came to her senses, she realised that there was not a moment to lose. She covered herself with a blanket and quickly packed a knapsack with food and other things. She glanced into the stables. In the far corner, standing unnoticed behind a tall, freshly made haystack, a long-maned horse was calmly chewing hay. It snorted happily at the sight of its mistress. Torebai's mother gave the horse some water, saddled up, snatched up her little son, and they galloped off at top speed. Bullets whizzed past them. They rode for miles without a backward glance, or any idea of where they were heading.

They galloped across the border and found themselves in China. They took refuge in a foreign land where no one threatened or bothered them. Some Kazakhs who had arrived earlier offered them work and a place to live. It seemed they might now be able to relax a little. But it wasn't to be. Torebai's mother never

---

[5] *aǧa* – here: a respectful form of address to an elder

recovered from the shock of her experience, which pushed her into a nervous breakdown. She could not get over it. Broken by grief, she would cry for days and nights on end, and she started at the slightest sound. Everything reminded her that this was a foreign, alien place that had been forced upon her, cutting her off forever from the far-distant past and her peaceful village life. It seemed to her that her husband and children were pottering about somewhere nearby; she could hear their voices all around her. Her health declined dramatically. Her eyes were sunken and swollen with tears; she was almost blind. Even the presence of her son and daughter-in-law raising her grandchildren did not bring her to her senses. Her brief moments of joy alternated with spells of despair. When in a frenzy of madness, she was blind and deaf to everyone and everything around her.

The monotonous days dragged drearily on. Torebai suppressed his feelings, because men weren't supposed to cry. His endless grief turned him into a stone statue. As soon as he was alone, he would weep noisily, furiously cursing the land he had been forced to leave, unable to move on from what had happened. His ears rang with the sound of the bullets whistling past, and his head with the question, "How did they not catch up with us?"

Torebai's mother, and his wife, and Torebai himself are long dead, and his children and grandchildren are scattered far and wide. Only rarely do they come to visit the graves of their loved ones.


3.

Meanwhile, Abish Ata and his children were hiding in the reeds. They were out of sight: there was a wide strip of thick grass, taller than waist-height, a sea of different wildflowers and low-growing trees. Beyond the vegetation lay an impenetrable waterlogged marsh. They had been forced into a corner: whether they went deeper into hiding, or stayed where they were, or came out, death was inevitable. Red Army soldiers armed with rifles were shouting, "Come out, Kazakhs!" as they fired into the reeds. Those bastards would abuse and rape young girls, gouge out eyes, cut off limbs, and kill. The terrified children cowered in the bushes, not daring to breathe in case the grass stirred, rippled by the wind, and gave them away. How many children there were, those filthy creatures never knew. When the sadists had had their fill of mocking and insulting them, they went on their way.

4.

What happened on that ill-fated day in 1929 stayed with Zauresh Apa[6] her whole life. She was a little girl when robbers burst into their home. They took their livestock, grain and all the supplies in the house. They mercilessly beat her parents to death. She and her brothers survived by fleeing to China. They endured a long and arduous journey into the unknown, shaking with fear and cold, a hungry existence. She found work as a servant with a wealthy family. Silently she grieved, her eyes clouded by a hazy veil of tears, a lump choking her throat. In the evenings she wept soundlessly as she prayed in memory of her loved ones. But it was there that she found happiness – she met her future husband, Murat Ata. They married and had children.
When the border with Kazakhstan opened, they packed hastily and returned to their homeland without a second thought.

5.

It has been unbelievably horrific even just to hear about the monumental tragedy that befell my people and the suffering they endured, let alone imagining the whole picture. What they went through was seared into their memories for the rest of their lives; the scars on their hearts never faded. Their families lived through the horrors of that time. We were shaken by their stories; they chilled us to the bone. My father-in-law is a very strong person, yet no one could fail to notice how much emotional pain he was in from these distressing memories. His voice shook and he could not hold back the tears.
I listened intently. Dry-eyed indifference was impossible. I was sick at heart, but my tears were mixed with admiration for the spiritual strength and resilience of our great people.

---

[6] *apa* – grandmother

As I write down the stories I heard, my eyes are wet once more and the lump has returned to my throat. I doubt that anyone could hear these stories and remain unmoved.

The award that Tynybek Ata had received from the tsar disappeared in 1929 after the Red marauders carried out their pogrom in the *aul*. In February 2020 my husband, a direct grandson of Tynybek Ata, sent a registered letter to His Holiness Patriarch Kirill of Moscow and all Rus asking him for "help with locating archival records concerning the award to my grandfather Tynybek". In May 2020 we received the following reply:

*Dear Zhanakhmet,*

*CHRIST IS RISEN!*

*The Patriarch of Moscow and all Rus has received your letter requesting archival information on your grandfather.*

*This is to let you know that no information on your grandfather Tynybek has been found in the Archive of the Moscow Patriarchate of the Russian Orthodox Church.*

*During the years when the Russian Orthodox Church was persecuted by militant atheists, hundreds of thousands of innocent priests, clergy and laypeople suffered and many monasteries, convents and churches were demolished. The Church's archives shared the same fate: some were nationalised and transferred to the appropriate Russian Federation state archives, but many were simply destroyed and irrevocably lost and cannot be restored.*

*The following state archives may be able to assist you in your search:*

- *The Russian State Historical Archive (RGIA), 36, Zanevsky Prospect, St Petersburg 195122. Tel. +7 (812) 438-5520.*
- *The State Historical Archive of the Russian Federation (GARF), 17, Bolshaya Pirogovskaya, Moscow 119992. Tel. +7 (495) 580-88-61.*

*You may also find it helpful to visit the Russian Archives website (www.rusarchives.ru).*

*I wish you and your family good health and spiritual peace. May the Lord keep you in His care!*

*Yours sincerely,*

*Father Alexei Kharlamov*
*Assistant Administrator, Correspondence Department*
*Moscow Patriarchate*

КАНЦЕЛЯРИЯ
СВЯТЕЙШЕГО ПАТРИАРХА
МОСКОВСКОГО И ВСЕЯ РУСИ

115191, Москва, ул. Даниловский вал, д. 22
Тел.: (495) 958-03-44
Факс: (495) 114-21-12

№ 01/2373

« 21 »        05        2020г.

Республика Казахстан,

Умирзакову Ж.Т.

Уважаемый Жанахмет,
ХРИСТОС ВОСКРЕСЕ!

В адрес Патриарха Московского и всея Руси Кирилла поступило письмо, в котором Вы запрашиваете архивные сведения о Вашем деле.

Сообщаю Вам, что в Архиве Московской Патриархии Русской Православной Церкви сведений о Вашем деле Тыныбеке не найдено.

В годы богоборческих гонений на Русскую Православную Церковь пострадали невинно сотни тысяч священно- и церковнослужителей, простых мирян, были разрушены многие монастыри и храмы. Эта же участь постигла и церковные архивы: часть из которых была национализирована и передана в соответствующие государственные архивы Российской Федерации, а многие архивы были просто уничтожены, безвозвратно утеряны и уже не подлежат восстановлению.

Возможно, в поиске необходимых сведений Вам помогут в следующих государственных архивах:

- Российский Государственный Исторический Архив (РГИА): 195112, г.Санкт-Петербург, Заневский проспект, д. 36. Тел.: +7(812) 438-5520.
- Государственный Исторический Архив Российской Федерации (ГАРФ): 119992, г. Москва, Большая Пироговская, д. 17. Тел.: +7(495) 580-88-61

Также Вам может оказаться полезным посетить сайт «Архивы России» (http://www.rusarchives.ru).

Желаю Вам и Вашим близким крепкого здоровья и мира душевного.

Храни Вас Господь!

С уважением,
референт Отдела по работе
с письмами Московской Патриархии

иерей Алексий Харламов

We are grateful to Father Alexei for responding. We have not given up hope that the records will be found.

6.

In 1926, the parents of my mother-in-law – my second mother – also found themselves in a foreign land as a result of brutal Stalinist harassment and oppression. They were educated and quite well-off people. They came from a clan of *biis*[7]. Her grandfather sat in court as a judge: he heard the local people's disputes, sorted out their problems, and resolved legal and land-related issues. He was greatly respected for his profound knowledge of history, his fairness and his skilful oratory. My mother-in-law inherited her grandfather's abilities.

On the face of it, they were in a foreign country, living with people who were foreigners to them. Yet no one humiliated them, or talked down to them, or prevented them from living and working there. A foreign land gave them refuge. Most importantly, they could live like human beings, abiding by the local customs. In their own native land, the Stalinist scum would not let them live their lives.

7.

My mother's grandfather lived in a village named Kapal. He was a prosperous farmer: he owned horses and a *qymys*-house and sold *qymys*[8]. He was ruthlessly persecuted by the secret police, the Cheka.

My mother used to reminisce about the deported Volga Germans who lived with her family in their home and worked on the collective farm. They were always being followed, since they were forbidden to leave their place of residence.

My mother's father, my *ata*, fought in the Second World War. A letter arrived to say that he had been killed in action. My mother's mother, my *apa*, was left with four young children – the youngest was under two. Ata had died defending our common Motherland, yet no help from that Motherland was

---

[7] *bii* – people's judges
[8] *qymys*, previously spelled *kumys*– fermented mare's milk

forthcoming. Such was the Stalinist regime. They got on with life as best they could.

The returning soldiers were rewarded by the state for their part in the victory, while the families of those who had been killed were pushed aside. How was this possible? Was it fair to honour some and forget others? After all, they were all fighting for the same state.

---

Tynybek Ata, who had refused to yield when his Russian neighbours tried to persuade him to flee to China, and when the Englishmen invited him to go with them to England, was brutally murdered by Stalin's henchmen in his native land.

These are just some of the stories about people who refused to submit to the iron rules of Stalin's bloody regime and attempted to change their lives. They will always remember that time. Circumstances forced them to flee from their native land, the land of their forefathers. These circumstances were brought about by Stalin's "infallible" servants. Who gave them the right to dispose of other people's lives? What did these subhumans do to an entire ethnic group? People don't flee their country if they have a good life there. Were these ordinary people supposed to stay and wait for death? Who did Stalin and his underlings think they were? Gods? Angels made flesh?

Brutal oppression, unfounded persecution, vicious attacks and intolerable socioeconomic conditions prompted millions of families to leave their homeland. So many Kazakhs were forced to wander, spending their lives and their strength in the struggle for survival...

Our ancestors endured so much hardship and stress. They were tortured in the most sophisticated ways, bullied mercilessly, treated with the utmost contempt. The Kazakhs suffered constant threats and brutality, draconian punishments and humiliating abuse. The Stalinist authorities ignored their pleas for help. Fighting back was beyond them. Everything they held most dear – family, friends, homeland – had been taken away from them. How much of this sort of discrimination could they bear? Life had become unsafe – that was why Kazakhs left the land of their birth, the land that had nourished them. After being forcibly expelled, scattered across different countries and resettled in foreign lands, they did not forget their historic roots, but preserved their language, faith and culture. Generations change, life changes, but our people's precious treasures – our traditions, culture and heritage – have endured.

Today, when we hear about acts of inhumanity committed by terrorists, we feel outraged and call for them to be severely punished. Who, then, will call out the secret police agents (NKVD) and the people's commissars for their actions? These people ruthlessly murdered millions of people in quick succession during the years of Stalin's reign, from tiny babies to grey-haired old men; they caused a bloodbath. What were their feelings as they did so? They must have had parents, brothers, sisters, families and children of their own. Or were they iron executioners, devoid of heart and soul?

**PART TWO**

1.

After the end of the Civil War and the institution of Soviet power, there was a huge number of orphans and vulnerable young people across the country. Abandoned to the mercy of fate, they drifted from place to place, hungry, ragged and homeless. In 1926, children's homes were opened in Russia. The conditions there were worse than in prison. Children would run away, preferring to fend for themselves. It was a desperate existence. 85% of them made bad choices, did stupid things, went off the rails. Little children were dying in the street, or robbing, stealing and thieving to get food, ending up behind bars. The leader of the Soviet government, Joseph Vissarionovich Stalin, was ruthless in every respect, devoid of any compassion or empathy. He reinforced his style of political leadership throughout the Soviet Union and toughened up legislation, employing intimidating methods of deterrence. Any dissenters who did not accept his methods were ruthlessly suppressed by force, repressed or shot. The official story was that it was bandits who were being killed and criminals who were being punished. It was difficult to work out exactly what a convicted person had been charged with or was suspected of doing. The theft of two loaves of bread was regarded as embezzlement of socialist property and treated as a criminal offence. "Enemies of the people" and their children and "delinquent" homeless orphans were judged in the same way. Without protocol. Punitive measures and unendurable punishments were meted out to children as young as twelve. Minors were given lengthy sentences for petty thefts and trivial offences, regardless of whether there might have been any justification for their actions and heedless of their heartrending cries and pleas for mercy. Juveniles were not held separately from adults – they were thrown into prisons and labour camps with appalling regulations and unwritten rules intended for hardened criminals. Millions of lives mangled and broken...

2.

After Soviet rule took hold in Kazakhstan, political persecution intensified. Stalin believed that the Kazakh people, as an ethnic group, did not fit into the large-scale industrial structure that was then being established. The bloodthirsty dictator took a keen interest in the fertile Kazakh lands. He was obsessed with the idea of forcibly confiscating these lands from the Kazakhs "for the good of the state" and either resettling the Kazakh people in uninhabitable regions or even getting rid of them altogether. These thoughts of conquest, conceived by a sick mind, would not leave him alone. And so he unleashed a bloody terror. His policy of collectivisation, as it was called, was directed against the Kazakhs' traditional way of life and, Stalin believed, would result in the total suppression of the Kazakh people.

The crude arbitrariness and unwarranted brutality in Kazakhstan provoked outrage among the people and stirred up discontent. The situation turned from panic to chaos. This could not go on for much longer. The people exploded. Across the republic, now here, now there, mass ethnic and political uprisings broke out. There were over 300 civil disturbances demanding national liberation. The Red Army brutally punished not only the participants who resisted them, but innocent bystanders as well – anyone who fell into their hands.

The First Secretary of the Central Committee of the Communist Party of Kazakhstan from 1925 to 1933 was the murderer Filipp Isayevich Goloshchyokin. The leader of Kazakhstan that Stalin appointed was an outsider who had absolutely no connection with the Kazakhs. The top job was given to a merciless executioner whose hands were already bloodstained: he had been one of the group of thugs who organised the shooting of the Russian royal family. He was also one of the key implementers of Stalin's vile plan to seize all livestock from the Kazakhs, thereby taking control of their nomadic lifestyle so that the Kazakhs themselves would perish. Something must have happened to these all-conquering aggressors that messed with their heads and damaged their values. Or maybe not – maybe their heads had always been messed up and they had never valued anyone or anything, and this came to the surface when they gained power? Perhaps this was the outward expression of their soullessness? Was it just the way the powers-that-be used the the weak to test their strength?

The ruthless policy of the Soviet regime led to genocide. These foul bloodsuckers did not regard the Kazakhs as human. They imbued them with timidity, meekness and submissiveness. Taking advantage of their powerlessness and aware of their own impunity, they bullied the Kazakhs in every possible way, behaving revoltingly, talking down to them with icy contempt. Now I realise that their haughty condescension, rudeness and arrogance highlighted their backwardness and lack of culture. But back then they were regarded as the "masters of the universe". We can scarcely imagine how terrifying and unpredictable these so-called masters of the universe were. Like Stalin, they opted for a zero-war tactic. To avoid problems, they unleashed aggression in an attempt to repress and subdue. It was easier for them to ignore the fact that Kazakhs were starving, suffering and dying than to face the truth, acknowledge the tragedy and the people's pain, and help them to return to their former way of life. Such a brutal and contemptuous attitude towards an entire ethnic group is surely not ethically acceptable. The scope of their ambition is astonishing. They crossed the line of what is acceptable.

Stalin made life intolerable for the Kazakhs, squeezed them out in every possible way, discriminated against them and forced them out of society. In this way he planned on achieving the total physical annihilation of the Kazakhs as an ethnic group.

At that time any discussion of the famine was categorically prohibited and rigorously policed by the state. The famine was not acknowledged. Documentary evidence of the death rates was carefully disposed of. Soviet censorship did not permit the dissemination of any information concerning this unwelcome topic, and there were harsh penalties for any attempts to publicise it. Our parents were therefore reluctant to keep the tragic past alive in their memories and share stories of what had happened to their people and their loved ones. To this day, there are huge gaps in the history of the famine and much remains undisclosed. The subject is neglected, mentioned hardly anywhere, and then only in passing. People would rather not talk about it. An accurate count has become more difficult. The figures in the official published statistics are skewed; moreover, they vary enormously. There is huge variation in the totals. A fabrication of history. It is difficult to reconstruct the chain of events and put together a complete historical picture of the past. Information is limited and divorced from reality; genuine information is hard to find. Any documents that cast even the slightest aspersion on the Stalinist era were removed from the archives. Anything that the Stalinists considered unnecessary was immediately burned. They reformatted everything the way they wanted it. That goes without saying…

The manmade famine or Holodomor also affected well-off Russian peasants, Volga Germans and Cossacks. They were hounded and banished for their loyalty to the tsarist army. There was also a Holodomor in the Volga region and Ukraine. The Ukrainian people has also gone through more than its share of suffering and heartbreak. But the famine was harshest, most harrowing and most catastrophic in Kazakhstan, where unprecedented violence and atrocities were artificially begun not in the 1930s, as stated in the available sources, but round about 1928. Stalin, the chief architect and instigator of every evil, was already aware even then of the scale of his plan. The clear intention was to totally destroy the Kazakh economy and to wipe the Kazakh people, along with their religious, historic and cultural traditions and customs, off the face of the earth. There is an abundance of contradictory facts and unconfirmed evidence.


3.

Not all Kazakhs led a nomadic lifestyle, as some writers have stated, claiming that the Kazakhs merely roamed about and pastured their animals. They also settled on land, where they farmed and kept livestock, sowed grain crops and grew fruit trees. I can state this with confidence based on our parents' reminiscences.

The land that had belonged to their ancestors stretched from Lake Balkhash to the Tarbagatai mountains. They themselves lived in the Ayaguz district in East Kazakhstan. In Tespakan, their *aul*, there were blacksmiths who made horseshoes, saddles, ploughs and tools for haying in their smithies, and master carpenters who made yurts, windows and doors for houses, light carts and other essential items. In early or late October, depending on the weather conditions, the herdsmen would leave to spend the winter on the shore of Lake Balkhash, near the mouth of the river Ayaguz. The locals would repair their homes and sheepfolds to insulate them against the cold, lay in stocks of animal feed, and mine salt. The salt was loaded onto camels and transported to South Kazakhstan, Tashkent and Samarkand.

In spring, the lambing season would begin. The sheep farmers would be kept busy as the new lambs added to their herds.

In early summer people dispersed: some to cultivate grain crops and make hay with which to feed the animals in winter, and some went away to the *jailyau*. A *jailyau* is an ideal place for livestock grazing and a wide-open space to relax in. The natural landscape is magnificent. Under the blazing mountain sun, with an abundance of rain and wind, in heat and cold, in the vast meadows, they pastured their animals, producing butter, *qaimaq*[9], soured cream, *airan*[10], *irimşik*[11], *qürt*[12], *qymys*, *sür et*[13], animal skins, meat, cheese, sausages (still in demand in many countries of the world today) and wool. They made felt carpets or *koşma*[14] for their yurts and sewed leather boots, camel-wool blankets, pillows and handicrafts.

In mid-August the herdsmen would drive the animals to Tespakan. The vegetation was lush and fertile, with tall reed

---

[9] *qaimaq* – a dairy product similar to clotted cream, made by skimming the cream off cooled boiled milk; later *qaimaq* began to be made using a special tool called a separator

[10] *airan* – a drink made from fermented milk, water and salt

[11] *irimşik* – an indulgent dairy product with a naturally sweet taste, with no added sugar, somewhere between curd cheese and hard cheese

[12] *qürt* – small balls of naturally dried sour cheese

[13] *sür et* – smoked meat

[14] *koşma* – a handmade felt carpet that provides insulation against both summer heat and winter cold and protects against poisonous insects. It is made by felting coarse sheep's wool from the autumn shearing and lasts for many years

thickets. Wild boar and deer grazed there together with the herds of sheep, horses, cows and camels. Interestingly, they all grazed together in their own little families; no one bothered anyone else, and all the animals remained safe and unharmed.

## 4.

Incidentally, six thousand years ago the Kazakhs were the first people to work and make articles out of leather, metal, stone, wood and bone. They were also the first people to domesticate and ride horses, and the first to make and drink *qymys*. Evidence for this has been found in excavations across the vast territory of Kazakhstan. While investigating the environs of Kazakhstan, archaeologists uncovered sizeable ancient settlements. The artefacts they found included fragments of extremely rare structures, the remains of horses and cows, tools, sanitation and hygiene items, leather goods, silver cutlery and tea services, bronze, wooden and clay vessels and other household utensils. The shards of pottery bore traces of milled grain and *qymys*. The composition of the latter was noted as being similar to modern-day *qymys*. Among the household items it was possible to recognise clothes such as long fur coats, women's waistcoats embroidered with gold beads in beautiful *oyu*[15] patterns, robes decorated with colourful embroidery, and leather-soled shoes.

These original finds, now on display in museum collections, showed that people farmed, made handicrafts, bred horses and grew crops many thousands of years ago in these places.

More than eight Golden Men – the remains of Saka warriors dressed in golden headdresses, gold-embroidered clothes and shoes – have been discovered in the course of archaeological excavations in Kazakhstan.

---

[15] *oyu* – traditional Kazakh ornament

The "Golden Man" discovered in 1969-1970
on the banks of the river Issyk, 53.5 km from Almaty

The garments are skilfully embroidered with delicate gold plates and discs in the shape of snow leopards, tigers, horses and other animals. Gold earrings with turquoise pendants, massive rings and various gold artefacts were also discovered – exquisite jewellery of the finest workmanship. The warrior's armour – an iron sword with a golden hilt and an iron dagger – and his horse's precious metal-plated harness and horseshoes demonstrate the development of metalworking in those far-off times when metal was still considered a rarity. These extraordinary finds of huge cultural significance confirm the sophistication of our ancient ancestors' civilisation.

Tandoor ovens – an essential attribute of the Kazakh household – have been found in the ruins of ancient cities in Central and South Kazakhstan. They are thought to date back to 400-300 BC. This provides further proof that the Kazakhs were growing grain crops even then.

There is also clear physical evidence that Kazakhs were engaged in agriculture in the 19th century: on 9 May 1840, Kazakh farmers near the river Karakol in the Ayaguz steppe stumbled upon an ordinary stone chondrite meteorite weighing 2.788 kg. The meteorite is kept in the collection of the USSR Academy of Sciences Meteorite Committee in Moscow[16].

5.

Now for a curious and not insignificant fact that I cannot leave out. There used to be a young naturalists' centre in the Auezov district of Almaty. It was opened in 1937. Now the "young naturalists" have been taken under the wing of the city's Palace of Schoolchildren. A new sign has appeared at the entrance that reads: "Palace of Schoolchildren GKKP[17]: Environment and Biology Department".

---

[16] Source: Ye.L. Krinov, *A Brief Catalogue of Meteorites in the USSR as of 1 January 1976*, Meteoritika, 1976, Vol. 35

[17] GKKP – state-funded cooperative enterprise

This is a heritage centre "where vestiges of the city's history are preserved and looked after". The natural setting contains a lilac garden, various flower gardens, a petting zoo, a nursery for rare and endangered plants, a pinetum, a fruit and berry orchard, an arboretum, an orangery with rare specimens of tropical plants, a modular garden, rose garden, aviary and greenhouse. The Sievers apple tree (*malus sieversii*), rightly considered the progenitor of every apple on earth, is cultivated here, as are vegetables, arable crops and medicinal plants.

As well as seeing the amazing floral displays, visitors to the centre will learn many other curious and fascinating facts – for example, that tulips originate from Kazakhstan, not Holland, as some people think. In addition to club-based activities, the centre organises and holds celebrations, exhibitions, competitions, festivals and other citywide and national events thanks to the hard work and involvement of the young naturalists.

There are colourful advertisements all along the fence surrounding the centre:

"…we are now in the remarkable genetic centre of origin of wild apple trees" – Nikolai Vavilov, 1929, in the wild apple forests of Zaili Alatau;

"*Malus sieversii* is the progenitor of every apple tree on Earth";

"Scientists have established that the earliest edible sweet apples on our planet grew only in the picturesque regions of modern-day Kazakhstan.
The *malus sieversii* apple tree is 165 million years old".

Did you know, dear reader, that Kazakhstan is the birthplace of every apple in the world? And that each and every edible variety of apple in existence originated from the wild apple trees of Kazakhstan that spread throughout the world? "The celebrated Almaty *apporte*, whose fruit tastes 'sweeter than dreams', is rightly considered one of the symbols of Almaty, Kazakhstan's southern capital." I would like to add that the district centre of Urdzhar[18], in the foothills of the Tarbagatai mountains, vies with Almaty as a contender for the title of "birthplace of the apple". Nursultan Nazarbayev, the first president of Kazakhstan, noted that "It has been scientifically proven that the Alatau foothills are the 'historic birthplace' of apples and tulips. This is the place from which these modest but internationally significant plants gradually spread to every country in the world."

---

[18] Urdzhar is now the administrative centre of the Urdzhar district in the East Kazakhstan region.

Nikolai Vavilov, the outstanding scientist who instituted the study of world centres of origin of cultivated plants, left these notes while on a research expedition in the Zaili Alatau mountains: "…here we are in the remarkable genetic centre of origin of wild apple trees."

What a delicious treasure we have amidst the "wild orchards of the Zaili and Dzhungar Alatau mountains, the like of which is not found anywhere else on earth"!

"Recognition of the Kazakhstani apple tree began with the legacy of this great scientist, who found backing for the theory that cultivated plants had originated from wild varieties… The Dictionary of Biology published by the USSR Academy of Sciences dates the origin of the wild apple tree *malus sieversii* to 165 million years ago. The Kazakhs who lived in these foothills did not just sow grain crops; they also cultivated fruit trees from the best varieties of the Kazakh wild apple.

In antiquity, the Silk Route passed through these places. From there, the apple tree began to spread east and west with the caravans. The botanist Johann Sievers was the first person to draw attention to the local apple tree. On learning that somewhere… there was an unknown variety of these fruits, he set off for the Tarbagatai mountains. Sievers first described these apples in the Kazakh settlement of Urdzhar in 1796."

"Our mountains are the heartland of the origin of all the wild apple and apricot trees on earth… and the area in which we live is utterly unique: the mountain ranges prevented alien species of plants from creeping in, and our wild fruit-bearing forests survived in their original form."

Following extensive research and genetic testing, leading scientists have concluded that the world centre of origin of apple trees is Zhetysu[19]: "Scientific research has confirmed that the gene pool of our (Kazakhstani) apple trees is present in practically every apple tree variety in the world… The work of an English scientist named Jennifer proved that all two thousand

---

[19] Zhetysu means Seven Rivers in Kazakh. The seven rivers that give the district its name are the Ili, Karatal, Bien, Aksu, Lepsy, Koksu and Ayaguz

cultivars of apple in England originated from the Kazakh wild apple.

American scientists tested our wild apple in 23 laboratories in various climatic zones and established that the trees do not freeze in the cold, tolerate heat well, and are resistant to disease."

Experts have concluded from fossil discoveries that dinosaurs appeared on the earth around 243 million years ago and lived on every continent. They survived for about 180 million years and died out approximately 66 million years ago.

Picture the scene, dear reader, millions of years before our time: hideous gigantic creatures were roaming the earth, while "within the territory of modern-day Kazakhstan", delicious wild apple trees were growing, scenting the air with the untold beauty of their blossoms!

6.

The settled Kazakhs lived in towns and *auls*. They kept livestock; they grew wheat, rye and millet for their own consumption, plus oats and barley for animal feed; they mowed hay and stocked up for the winter. Their painstaking labour laid the foundation for the entire country's economy. Kazakhstan was a bottomless feeding trough of raw materials for the Kremlin. The proceeds from selling these were used to purchase the equipment needed for industrialisation from America. Russia obtained 80% of its meat from Kazakhstan, since Russia was considered a vitally important artery. It was incumbent on Kazakhstan to supply meat, grain and wool. In addition to the existing taxes the Kremlin thought up new ones, increasing every kind of levy on the population.

The Kazakhs were desperately hungry, yet there was no reduction in the enforced exactions, and any "surplus" food continued to be freighted out of Kazakhstan.

Under the guise of collectivisation, Stalin and his sidekicks deliberately and resolutely continued to push through their policy of annihilating the Kazakhs by eradicating all of their livestock through mass slaughter. Hiding behind Communist slogans such as "Workers of the world, unite!", "The party is our helmsman!" and "The people and the party are one!", they bled the Kazakhs dry, making life impossible for them.

To carry out their plans, they brought in a Russian squad of armed security forces. The villainous Bolsheviks would stop at nothing: like devastating invasions of vast hordes of voracious locusts, they swallowed up everything in one gulp. They cleaned out the cereal crops to the very last grain and seized livestock, agricultural produce and equipment for haymaking and ploughing, knowing that meat and grain were the Kazakhs' sole source of food, their livelihood. Across the whole Kazakh land, in the towns and the *auls*, the people's commissars ruled the roost, swooping down out of nowhere, pillaging, turning everything upside down. They were called "people's" commissars when in fact they were the people's deadliest enemies – terrorists, thieves and murderers. Their violence shattered the local people's peace and tranquillity. They would break into Kazakhs' homes, search in every nook and cranny, seize their assets and ransack the place. They didn't leave out a single house. They trawled the land looking for food. They would strip yurts and barns bare of grain and provisions, using up all that the family had stored, take precious jewellery from their trunks, and confiscate their cattle, while people were starving.

The likes of such raids have perhaps never been seen anywhere. A natural disaster – like an eruption of molten lava from a fire-breathing volcano, when the sky falls in, a pillar of smoke rises to a great height and an abyss opens up at your feet – is dreadful, but you understand that this is nature and we are powerless to stop it. Here, though, we have the human factor; these disasters were made by human hands. The swarm of Red vermin crushed everything in its path, then gloated triumphantly at the sight of the torments in which their victims perished. In desperate need, the Kazakhs endured terrible injustice, humiliation and brutality. Not all of the Kazakhs were meek and mild. Those who resisted and obstructed the barbarians in defence of their property were butchered on the spot: forced to their knees, their eyes were gouged out, parts of their skin were ripped off, salt was poured onto the wounds, and they were beaten to death.

Seeing the attackers savagely executing their grown-ups, stuffing sacks full of their grain, and driving away their cows, sheep, horses and camels, the terrified children screamed and sobbed, distraught and helpless. At a tender age, they experienced the pain and fear of witnessing the deaths of many of their family members and friends. The Bolsheviks were unmoved by the violent weeping and hysterical screams. Any confiscated livestock that they could not take away with them were shot right in front of the starving people and buried in pits. Then the dead animals were even guarded until they were rotten and stinking so that no one could dig them up. The population was left entirely without food, with no meat and no bread, until the meat had rotted in the pits and the sacks of wheat were soaked through and useless from the rain.

The consequences of all the blunders made by their incompetent rulers fell to the people to deal with. Every home and every family were stricken by an inconsolable grief. Families were reduced to poverty. People in every region of Kazakhstan were subjected to politically motivated harassment. This was how the Bolsheviks tried to force the Kazakhs to submit to Soviet authority. There was no regard for tiny babies, or breastfeeding mothers, or frail elderly people. Deprived of food and left to face hunger and cold, all were condemned to inevitable death – families, people of all ages, the sick, the weak, the vulnerable. Only Stalin and his mindless henchmen could have done such a thing. Everywhere the foul scent of death hung in the air, and bloodstained corpses lay side by side in the streets. There were some courageous individuals who wrote to Kalinin and other officials in Moscow describing the challenging situation in the Kazakh republic, informing them that since the Kazakhs' livestock had been confiscated, people had nothing to eat and were starving to death. But there was no response to their letters. The feeling was that nobody cared. No one was in a hurry to help these people in distress, no one seemed to hear or see, as if they were behind a curtain. Yet all the high-handed actions of Stalin's representatives, sidestepping the urgent need to address the people's concerns, were carried out at Stalin's behest, and his entourage would have been well aware of his heinous plans. There are claims on paper that food aid was allocated to the starving people, but it never reached the intended recipients for various reasons: remoteness, lack of roads, insufficient transport, "attempted misappropriation". Even if these claims made by representatives of the state bureaucracy are accepted as fact, what is beyond doubt is that there was no urgency involved; they were just going through the motions, purely for reporting purposes. Party bureaucrats excelled at drawing up accounts and manipulating figures. People were dying, and they received no help.

Stalin bled the Kazakhs dry and abandoned them to the inevitable disaster of the devastating famine. America was in an economic depression at the time, and it was to America that Stalin sent the meat and wheat that had been confiscated from the Kazakh people. Was Franklin D. Roosevelt (President of the USA from March 1933 to April 1945) aware of the price that had been paid for this Soviet humanitarian aid? I venture to suggest that in all likelihood he was not. It was all hushed up.

7.

The Stalinist werewolves within the ranks of Party, state and military officials went on the attack like packs of mad dogs with bared fangs; there was no chance of survival. To the ordinary people, they represented death. "Faced with the threat of starving to death, the Kazakhs were forced to flee." In terror at the impending disaster, fearful and despairing, ordinary civilians left their homeland to save themselves from starvation and mass repressions, drawing on the spirit of their ancestors, traditions and time. They could not accept their bitter fate. Totally isolated, deprived of all rights and livelihood, backed into a corner, these wounded souls fled in fear and panic from their *auls* in every direction. It is difficult to arrive at the exact number of Kazakhs who left at this time. Whole villages were wiped out. The borders were surrounded with numerous convoys; cordons were established all over the place; the NKVD would not let those fleeing the famine enter the city and would fire at them in an attempt to stop them.

Some struggled to the death. Exhausted and emaciated, they died on the way as they were approaching the city. They died not from malnutrition, but starvation. By some miracle, the survivors kept on walking. They walked through rain and through snow. When the snow melted, dead bodies were revealed all over the steppe. The dusty roads were lined with young women clutching swaddled babies to their breasts, children with bellies swollen with hunger, shrivelled-up old men. The land cried out in pain, soaked with blood and tears. Once-thriving districts that had been teeming with life had become a deathly kingdom reigned over by an ominous, sepulchral silence; not a single living soul was left. The endless steppes were strewn with human bones. The Kazakhs' beloved native steppes, where they had grown up, pastured their animals and grown their bread, had become their final resting place – their graves.

Those refugees who managed against the odds to cross the border into the neighbouring regions of Russia were clearly not expected. Russians refused to accept them, would not let them into their homes and locked their doors firmly against them. Some were following the local authorities' instructions that all Kazakhs should be immediately sent back; others were acting on their chauvinist-nationalist views. Then they hurled insults and profanities after the refugees. Weakened by the journey, hungry, cold and half-dead, they would collapse on the doorsteps, by the wayside, in the streets. Those who somehow managed to move on would be jeered at, violated, even killed, and the derelict buildings where they found temporary shelter were set on fire. The groans of the dying could be heard all around, and the muddy ground was smeared with long trails of blood. Bony, outstretched hands, a muffled rasping sound, mud, mutilated corpses lying in the storm-frozen scum, scraps of clothing…

Mothers had to watch their children die. Unable to stand the pain, they would lose their minds, cradling their dead children and singing lullabies to them…

How could Stalin deliberately cause the Holodomor? No mother can endure her child's crying for one second; her heart feels like bursting, so that she runs over and holds them close, comforts them, gives them something to eat. But what can a woman do if her milk has dried up because she herself hasn't eaten? Little children died in their mothers' arms, screaming until they choked. How can anyone get over that?

In our own day, when I hear about starving children in Africa, the image that comes to my mind is a Kazakh mother with her baby dying at her dried-up breast. My heart will not be comforted, and I weep bitter tears.

To this day I have an indescribable horror of racial and ethnic inequality, the infringement of human rights and freedoms, mistreatment and cynical indifference. Social inequality is, alas, the norm in society, differing only in its extent. If you think about it, no ethnic group, religion, race, culture or language is superior to any other. There should be no dominance. Everyone is equal. It doesn't matter whether your skin is black or white, or whether you follow Christianity, Islam, Buddhism or Judaism.

I treat people with respect; I value integrity and honesty. I'm against dividing people according to different characteristics and against physical or verbal abuse in any country.

To destroy a world of kindness, you don't need any special means of destruction. It's nothing to do with them – it's about those who use violence to get rid of people who are of no use to them. The world is turning into a world of predators. There are all kinds of rabble-rousers, nationalists and provocateurs who pose a very real threat to stability. They are full of nastiness: implacable hatred, deep-rooted bitterness, unconcealed envy, outrageous bare-faced lies, cunning and guile, relentless and insatiable greed. They use other people to achieve their ends, stirring up the weak rather than doing the job themselves. This is an evil that must be rooted out. We need to join together to fight against this evil and expose this layer of parasites. There have been those who tried to fight alone – it didn't work. One by one they were easily broken like the twigs of a broom. No one can break a solid bundle. We can only root out this evil by working together. We need to talk and write about this over and over like a broken record, and to argue in order to warn people about acting without thinking and discourage them from doing wrong. Not be singing their praises the whole time. And we can bring back those lost unchanging values, bring back the world of kindness, a life without deception and betrayal, dirty tricks and lies, cruelty and suffering. Whatever happens, we must remain human beings with heart, honourable and equally fair to everyone, holding onto our human qualities, warmth, spirit of unity and moral values, standing up to evil and violence, not undermining the social conscience, and maintaining mutual respect in civil society. We have to change the way we treat people, to live at peace with our conscience, with kindness, respect, love and compassion. We must learn to do "that which is wise, good, and eternal", to rebuild and not destroy.


8.

Stalinist brutality condemned the Kazakhs to wander endlessly, fearing for their lives. Years later, it became known that Kazakhs were scattered throughout the Soviet Union and all over the world, having managed to evade increased militarised security and walked hundreds of miles. Only a handful of them made it.

Our parents told us that the 20th century wasn't the only time when Kazakhs had left their homeland; further back in history, there were times when they had been driven to extreme desperation and forced to protect their families. Then, too, they had been unable to submit to violence and abuse, brutal beatings and agonising torture, the degradation of their honour and dignity, and other forms of unlawful coercion and oppression from the powers-that-be.

Kazakhs reluctantly found themselves in foreign lands, far from their historic homeland, weak with hunger and thirst, utterly exhausted by the long and arduous crossing, and living in limbo. They found shelter in Turkmenistan, Uzbekistan, Turkey, Iran, China, India, Afghanistan, Germany, the UK. The descendants of these Kazakh migrants remained in the countries that had once taken in their parents and grandparents. The survivors trembled as they recalled what they had been through; their hearts ached from the loss of their loved ones, and their eyes were filled with sorrow, anxiety and despair. Their shared grief united them. Worn out emotionally and physically, weeping and wailing, their tears washed away the grief that came flooding back. They sobbed violently; they didn't hold back from expressing their feelings in public. That period of their lives had left its mark in their lifeless eyes and lined faces, where their pain was clear to see. Their relatives and fellow villagers alike had left their *auls*. They settled in new places – in other countries, foreign lands – and lived on with cautious hopes of returning.

Later, after listening to these stories, I came across the published findings of people who had conducted research into the causes of the dramatic decline in the Kazakh population. In attempting to find an explanation, they leaned heavily on the lack of information on the Holodomor. Without any grounds for doing so, these researchers had concluded that an epidemic had been raging in the Kazakh areas, which were largely populated by decrepit old people and small children, and that aid from the authorities had not got through due to the danger of infection. According to them, disease and lack of sanitation were the main reason for the loss of life. How could they have got this so unashamedly wrong? This is utter nonsense – a cobbled-together fabrication. Reasoning ought to have logic behind it. There is no historical or legal foundation for these people's denials, no grounds for their claims. We must be guided by irrefutable facts, not falsehoods and fantasies produced by over-active imaginations.

These researchers were relying on superficial analyses and thereby seeking to justify Stalin's regime. Ignoring convincing proofs and incontrovertible evidence, they deliberately closed their eyes to the obvious and gave their own assessment of the situation. There is no incentive for them to bring the truth about the Kazakhs out into the open and present it for public consumption. They put their own spin on it to mislead and confuse people, and they impose their twisted interpretation on the rest of the world. The most likely reason why they refuse to acknowledge the Holodomor is that then the puppet-masters would have to be held to account for chaos and discrimination, diabolical evil and human suffering, millions of deaths and deliberate distortion of the facts. There were no epidemics and there was no lack of sanitation. The Kazakhs worked in the fields and raised their livestock. They were prosperous, and their living conditions were clean, cosy, warm and comfortable. Here we could do with a reminder that the Kazakhs invented household soap (made from animal fat, mint and other ingredients) and the practice of soaking dirty linen in a hot salt solution long, long ago.

The Holodomor was artificially engineered by Stalin with the aim of wiping the Kazakhs as an ethnic group off the face of the earth.

It is true that the famine also coincided with natural climate disasters such as drought, early frosts and other events.

"Based on the historical evidence, it can be stated that the first Famine on the Kazakh steppe struck in 1918-19, immediately following the October Revolution. The main cause was the policy of war communism. The people were stripped of everything in order to supply food to the Red Army.

The second stage of the Famine began in 1921-22."

Our parents described how looting and banditry by both Reds and Whites caused the Kazakhs to go hungry during those years. It was impossible for them to live in peace. If Reds were approaching an *aul*, the people there, hoping for mercy and clemency, would hang out a scrap of red fabric to symbolise the red flag. If Whites appeared on the horizon, they would use white fabric. Then the barbarians would be much more lenient and there would be less plunder. They would empty the coffers, stuff their bellies until they could eat no more, and carry food supplies away with them.

But occasionally people would misidentify the armies and put up the wrong flag. Then there was no leniency. A slip like that would cost them their lives. The furious bandits would punish them severely: they would burn the *aul* to the ground and torture the people, who had nowhere to run.

So many settlements were turned into "empty, burned-out deserts" after an attack by these unbridled vandals.

The number of people who died is estimated at 3 million. But this is not even close to correct – the true number is far greater.

Arguments continue to this day regarding the exact total number of victims of the Holodomor in the 1920s and 30s. There are "major discrepancies with the actual data". The figures are clearly understated. Some people resort to forging data, using every trick in the book. Most researchers give only rough estimates of the losses. They pull the wool over the international community's eyes. "The exact number of lives lost has yet to be established."

The mass famine in Kazakhstan in the late 1920s and early 1930s was artificially engineered by Stalin. It was a deliberate crime against humanity on his part. His policy of Russification involved not merely exterminating the Kazakhs physically, but also eradicating their language, religion and culture.

Researchers have painted a distorted picture. They appear to have been unaware of the fact that no one was permitted to mention the Holodomor in those days. It was a completely taboo subject. There was a very strong bias at work among Soviet citizens: no one went against the authorities. The orders given by leaders on various levels had a magic power that affected the people's consciousness, forcing them to keep silent. Lies upon lies. To this day people live in slavish obedience and blind submission to a powerful elite. No one has the right to go against them. "The slave mentality is deeply rooted in our consciousness." People just follow whatever signals they receive from above like ever-obedient programmed robots. Ordinary people are afraid to express their opinions in public. There is no debate. The older generation are still fearful for their families. This fear seems to be psychologically handed down – it's in the blood.

Prominent Kazakh government officials, public figures and literary pioneers who dared, despite the strict censorship and restrictions, to write openly to Stalin and other influential party leaders about the Holodomor were accused of nationalism by Stalin and imprisoned, sent to labour camps or shot. The incontrovertible evidence they provided was deliberately expunged from the records.

The cause of the Kazakhs' high death rate was in fact starvation, not disease. It was Stalinist persecution on a massive scale, chronic famine, forced expulsions and sheer desperation that made Kazakhs uproot themselves and run for the hills. If they were all sick and elderly people and children, how could they have independently travelled hundreds and thousands of miles beyond Kazakhstan? Groundless speculation like this needs debunking. People only say this sort of thing if they are proponents of Stalin's ideas. They heap praise on Stalin, seeing him as a symbol of the Soviet era, and defend his wickedness and treachery. Regrettably, Stalinism is still with us. You can still find prominent apologists of his who dream of restoring the Stalin era. Nazis who support Stalin and his ilk have not gone away. They had time to cover their tracks; they went underground and lay low for a while. 99% of Hitler's henchmen were punished, while Stalin's camouflaged themselves and melted into the crowd. They were never brought to justice. Stalin did not betray those who served him faithfully. He used to have inconvenient witnesses quietly executed so that they could not expose him. That was how his secrets were kept. Then there were those who claimed to be front-line veterans and became heroes. They amassed considerable fortunes and sauntered around the places they themselves had ruined. How come they had the right to go on living? Surely their camouflage didn't actually enable them to forget their own crimes against humanity?

9.

Some Russians hark back to the significant positive role Stalin played in their country's history and call him "the greatest leader of the last hundred years", "Russia's greatest ruler" and "the most outstanding political leader of the 20th century". They believe that "Stalin made Russia great."

According to Vladimir Putin, president of the Russian Federation, "Stalinism cannot be likened to Nazism... Despite all the monstrousness of the Stalinist regime, despite all the repressions, even despite whole ethnic groups being sent into exile, nonetheless the Stalinist regime never set out to exterminate particular ethnic groups." Putin says he is going to "keep on talking" about "Stalin's contributions to the victory over Nazism", insisting that "the undue demonisation of Stalin is a way of attacking the Soviet Union and Russia."

How can anyone accept Putin's claim that the bloody dictator did not set out to exterminate ethnic groups, given the unprecedented scale and scope of the repressions?

The Russian actor Aleksey Serebryakov has said that Russia's national idea is power, arrogance and rudeness. All the actions of the Russian leadership serve only to confirm that.

Stalin was a cold-hearted, belligerent man who believed he was always right and never listened to anyone. In my opinion, no one compares with him and Hitler. For monstrous inhumanity they have no equals. Hitler's fascism emerged during the years of the Second World War, at a time when Stalin was thinking up various plots and schemes before coming to power. Stalin overcame Hitler, and he outdid him. By the time Hitler was no longer leader of Germany, Stalin had built camps up and down the USSR, many in Siberia and Kazakhstan, to which he sent "delinquents" and their families to be brutally dealt with. I can't help wondering whether Hitler learned from Stalin. Hitler sent people to his camps, gassed them, and burned their half-frozen corpses. He used the ash as fertiliser. Stalin starved the prisoners in his freezing camps and they froze to death, dying of cold, malnutrition and disease. The whole world knows about Hitler and his crimes against humanity, and we have at least approximate data on the number of Jews he killed. Stalin's sadistic deeds are also common knowledge, but accurate statistics are nowhere to be found regarding the atrocities he visited on the Ukrainians, Jews, Germans, Kazakhs, Russians, Tatars, Koreans, people from the Caucasus, and other ethnic groups who lived in the USSR. The secret remains closely guarded to this day: a policy both misguided and misleading.

Take a moment, dear reader, to reflect on how you are feeling now. For my part, I feel fear, contempt, hatred, revulsion. Stalin was the scum of the earth – evil incarnate. What he did has left an indelible aftertaste of bitterness in our souls. His vile treachery towards an entire people is an outrage. There are serious problems with the veracity and safe preservation of historical documents regarding the dire situation of the Kazakh people. It's so important that we tell future generations about what actually happened and how. In the past, anyone who spoke or wrote about this was silenced. Who will speak up now? Who will expose the Stalin sympathisers? Which doors must we knock on in order to be heard? When will the day come when everything that has been done to our people will be laid bare?

The stories told about our Kazakh people are backed up by my father-in-law's accounts. This really is how it was. We are under an obligation to defend historical truth.

Communities were destroyed and an entire ethnic group was subjected to cruel accusations and persecution: robbed of all they had, sentenced to death, shot, sent to labour camps. Betrayed, impoverished and desperate, the Kazakhs were forced to migrate to unknown lands to escape Stalin's arbitrary despotism. As they searched for new places to live, they endured a desperate existence, travelling for months through pouring rain and driving snow, searing heat and bitter cold. Even once abroad, they were not guaranteed safety everywhere. Stalin's reach extended as far as China. Fearing brutality and harassment, some Kazakhs fled China, only to face a new danger in the Himalayas. Their route was blocked by some Tibetans, who stole their livestock and killed a number of people. The Kazakh men fought back against the Tibetans. Having lost over half of their number, the surviving Kazakhs crossed the mountains and entered India. Here they struggled to find housing and work, as they were not permitted to farm. Abandoned to the mercy of fate, they asked the Turkish consulate for help. Through the Red Cross, with help from the International Migration Fund, Turkey arranged travel by air and sea and welcomed the Kazakhs as if they were its own people. Turkey provided housing, land, livestock, credit – in short, made life possible. The help given by the Turkish authorities and the Turkish people was incomparable.

No one harassed the Kazakhs in their new homes, but not everyone could adapt to the new conditions. No matter how good their lives were, once Stalin was dead the Kazakhs living in China began to return to their homeland so that their children would not forget their roots. Some Kazakhs, fearing persecution and mistreatment by supporters of the Stalinist regime, remained in China and stayed in touch with their relatives. They began to return when Kazakhstan became a sovereign state.

---

For many good reasons, Kazakhs found themselves living outside their homeland and faced problems adapting to their new living conditions in foreign countries. The Kazakh diaspora in every country preserves its national identity and maintains links with its historic homeland.

Ethnic Kazakhs (*kandastar*) living abroad remain faithful to the traditions of their forefathers, regard the ancient customs as sacred, and preserve their spiritual and cultural heritage. Their Kazakh way of life is evident from their manner of speaking and the purity of their language (uncontaminated by foreign borrowings!), their belongings, the way they cook and serve meals, and the fact that they teach their children the secrets and ways of typically Kazakh crafts and applied art. We have noticed this whenever we visited such people.

10.

It was a period of demonic brutality. The savage atrocities perpetrated by Stalin and his henchmen send shivers down your spine, chill your soul, and break your heart. A terrifying picture of absolute lawlessness is taking shape. It was so easy to make false accusations and denunciations. Even an anonymous tip-off was sufficient. No one could deal with a false accusation. The Kazakhs as a people were bullied. Stalin was attempting to build a new society, and the best and brightest Kazakh minds had no place in it. They would only get in his way. So Stalin embarked on a physical purge. His pack of dogs sniffed everything out ahead of time. They hunted down the leaders and activists, identified them in advance, then pursued them and eliminated them wherever they were to be found. There was nowhere to hide from Stalin's network of informers: they would comb every nook and cranny. They used ostracism, surveillance, interrogations, secret provocations and misinformation. All of the most brilliant thinkers of the Kazakh nation without exception – the creative intelligentsia, politically shrewd, forward-thinking people who were unacceptable to the Soviet authorities – were arrested on trumped-up charges, imprisoned, sent to concentration camps to be "re-educated", or shot as "Enemies of the People" and "Traitors to the Motherland". They were humiliated in every possible way, suspended from their jobs, hounded out, disbarred from government bodies, denied representation in the authorities, and lured into all kinds of deadly traps. So many exceptional people and their families were destroyed.

Stalin's entourage and army were largely made up of illiterates, so they had no love for Kazakhs from erudite aristocratic backgrounds. They looked for any excuse to slander and defame them so as to clear all undesirables from their path; they locked up innocent scapegoats as and when they felt like it and pronounced death sentences without any investigation or trial. They were the judge and jury. They saw the Kazakhs as a threat to the social order. They were afraid that these incorruptible people, with their high spiritual and moral values, would lay claim to power. They punished their families too, restricting their rights and showing no mercy to their elderly parents, wives, young children or siblings. Why, you may ask? People were weeping in sorrow and writhing in agony. There was no cursing. Their powerlessness was expressed in a plaintive, long-drawn-out wail. Yet neither children sobbing their hearts out, nor heartrending cries for help, nor piteous lamentations could affect the spawn of Stalin. They were devoid of basic human qualities – fellow feeling, sympathy, compassion. They were twisted by revulsion and contempt. The slaughter and repression of the Kazakh elite was directly linked to the murderous policy of annihilating the entire Kazakh people. Stalin rained anger and paranoia down on anyone "dubious". By his standards they had no right to live. The lives destroyed cannot be counted.

Yet Stalin's "top-down" leadership system, which had committed such criminal acts (the Holodomor and repressions), did however attempt to substantially understate the scale of their barbarous crimes, and they totally destroyed most of the documentation. These Nazi criminals were craftier than any bandit. Hugely understated figures were given for the number of Kazakh victims of the brutal killings. The objectivity of the official data is extremely dubious. Certainly the 1937 population census was not properly carried out. Facts were twisted and made-up figures were plucked out of nowhere. An accurate headcount was unrealistic. The hypothesis that the census statistics were crudely falsified and incomplete is certainly not unsupported. Otherwise, how do you explain the fact that the population was supposedly counted in a single day – in the endless Kazakh steppes, with minimal literacy, transport and communications? How was it possible to complete a census within eight hours in the ninth largest country in the world by land mass? What was the number of people living in the regions where no inhabitants remained? Literacy levels were poor because the core members of the Kazakh political and creative elite, the highly qualified literate Kazakhs, had been purged by Stalin: some had been shot, some exiled, and some vanished without trace. When they were released from the hell of prison after long years of detention, they would come out as sick people, condemned to a martyr's death. Over 10 million people died between 1918 and 1941 (before the USSR entered the Second World War). By 1970, the indigenous Kazakh population made up less than a third of the population of Kazakhstan. I later read an article in the literary magazine *Prostor* in which editor-in-chief Valery Mikhailov described Stalin's Holodomor as "a terrible disaster that the republic lived through": "No other tragedy of this scale is known to world history." In December 2008 he wrote, "There is no documentary evidence of the horrific tragedy that befell the Kazakhs, the death of almost 40% of the population by starvation. The state archive contained no records relating to the famine. It's as if this disaster that struck Kazakhstan in the early 1930s never happened. Everything was either wiped clean, destroyed long ago, or hidden away in a massive cover-up."

The figure of 40% mentioned above was taken from the data originally available. It turned out to be falsified and a long way from the truth – which is that over half the population died, 70-80%. Inaccurate and unconfirmed statistics were given for political reasons. Other researchers use these made-up percentages. Here we have a blatant contradiction, with journalists going against their own conviction that "when it comes to history and politics, it's better not to read anything published in Russian" (as Russian publicist Dmitry Puchkov put it).

To fatally weaken the Kazakhs and sever the cultural and historic link between the generations, Stalin forced through reforms to the Kazakh writing system: the switch from Arabic to Latin script in 1928, and from Latin to Cyrillic in 1940. This was blatant mockery of an entire people! The change of alphabet and writing system and the adoption of new scripts replaced traditional values and held back the overall development of the Kazakh language. These linguistic experiments affected the development of Kazakh literature and cut it off from the rest of the world.

Nothing compares to the way the fate of the Kazakh people was crippled and mutilated. Stalin's radical transformations brought about huge demographic change. The population dropped precipitously. Ethnic Kazakhs were now a minority in their own republic. Stalin could afford to ruin Kazakhstan and drive an entire people to extinction, denying them all means of survival, subjecting them to inhuman torture and horrific conditions incompatible with life. There was no end to his atrocities; it is not possible to list them all. Far from preventing tragedy, he did all he could to make it happen. His sick mind had spawned the idea of eradicating the whole Kazakh people, and he brooded over it, working out a set of measures that would bring it to fruition. Neither pregnant women, nor breastfeeding mothers, nor tiny newborn babies that had just come into the world, nor hunchbacked old men made his heart so much as flinch. Is this normal? He was an emotional cripple, blind and deaf to human suffering, incapable of empathy or compassion. He did not regard anyone else as human. And who was he after all? Who brought this monster into the world?

Stalin and Goloshchyokin deliberately permitted serious excesses and callously destroyed millions of lives. How could anyone stand up for the defenceless against such executioners? Nothing would have stopped these vultures. I must emphasise that the Kazakh famine was instigated and perpetrated by Stalin himself. The Bolshevik Goloshchyokin was removed from his post in 1933.

On 21 January 1933, Levon Isayevich Mirzoyan took over from Goloshchyokin. Once again, Stalin had appointed one of his henchmen to govern the Kazakhs. But even this outsider, who had nothing in common with the Kazakh people and felt nothing for them, was horrified by the situation: "When I left Moscow I was sure the situation in Kazakhstan would be dire, but what I have seen here has gone beyond all my expectations."

Stalin's acolyte continued to implement his murderous policy of aggression in Kazakhstan, following the established process. "Mirzoyan facilitated the annihilation of the Kazakh intelligentsia."

There is evidence that Mirzoyan and Goloshchyokin exterminated over 126,000 Kazakh intellectuals. In fact, the number of people for whose deaths they are responsible is incalculable.

Goloshchyokin and Mirzoyan's actions were subsequently criticised. Stalin quickly got rid of them before they could expose him as a co-conspirator to justify themselves and mitigate their own culpability.

Stalin treated Goloshchyokin in the same way as he had Mirzoyan. Having personally sent them to carry out his criminal plans in Kazakhstan, he later purged them as inconvenient witnesses: Mirzoyan was shot on 26 February 1939 and Goloshchyokin in October 1941.

The deep scars that mark the fate of the Kazakh people cannot be washed away. We must never forget the "innocent victims of the unlawful Stalinist repressions". Millions of people disappeared into the camps. Those inmates who survived bore the indelible stamp of camp life. History is being rewritten and reworked, memories are being erased. There is no access to archive documents. Chaos reigned during those years: real criminals would go free for political reasons, while political actions were frequently classed as criminal offences. Even now, not everyone who was convicted on political grounds has been rehabilitated.

There were eleven correctional labour camps (Gulags) within the territory of Kazakhstan, the largest of which was Karlag (the Karaganda special regime camp). The others were Dalny, Stepnoi, Peschany, Kamyshlag, Aktyubinsk, Dzhezkazgan, Petropavlovsk, Kengir (special camp), Ust-Kamenogorsk, and ALZhIR, an acronym for the Akmola Camp for Wives of "Traitors to the Motherland". Over 5 million prisoners were held in the camps.

---

After the 1917 October Revolution, there were partisans in the mountains of Tarbagatai, in hiding from the White ataman Boris Annenkov. The brigade was made up of Cossack farmhands. They were fighting a guerrilla war with the Whites and anyone who opposed Soviet power. They looted Kazakh *auls* and murdered innocent civilians. They named their brigade the "Red Mountain Eagles". Between 1929 and 1935 they took part in the mass shooting of livestock in Zhanai. They fleeced desperate people escaping the Stalinist regime, who had already been bled dry.
When a collective farm was later founded in the Urdzhar district in East Kazakhstan (formerly Semipalatinsk), it was given that very name: Red Mountain Eagles.

11.
The bloodthirsty dictator and his demonic entourage had embarked on their policy of annihilating the Kazakh people and taking over their fertile, resource-rich lands. How come they

were free to do as they pleased? Who gave them the right to turn the lives of peaceful civilians upside down?

Following the expulsion of the Kazakhs and the depopulation of the territory they had vacated, a new workforce was brought in from central Russia and other republics. This was only the beginning. What devious schemes this Soviet-era executioner and despot intended to carry out next, only he knew. His plans were foiled by the war.

I was astonished to hear from our parents that prior to the Holodomor, ethnic Kazakhs also lived in the Volga region and in Orenburg, Saratov, Orsk, Tyumen, Omsk and other cities that I knew from my schooldays were considered Russian. My father-in-law debunked this idea, emphasising that the Kazakh origin of these places has been preserved in their names, although some names have been corrupted out of all recognition:

Orenburg – *Orynbor* in Kazakh, meaning "chalky place";

Saratov – *Sary tau* in Kazakh, meaning "yellow mountain";

Orsk – *Or qala* in Kazakh, meaning "valley town";

Kurgan – *Qorğan* in Kazakh, meaning "hill";

Tyumen – *Tömen* in Kazakh, meaning "low";

Tomsk – *Tomby* in Kazakh ("tom bolyp qatyp qalady"), meaning "ground stiff with frost";

Omsk – *Omby* in Kazakh ("ombalap juredi"), meaning "much snow falls";

Lake Baikal – *Baiköl* in Kazakh, meaning "rich lake".

The Chelyabinsk region, where a meteorite fell in February 2013, contains Lake Chebarkul – *Şūbarköl* in Kazakh, meaning "rippled lake";

Chelyabinsk also has a district named Kunashak – *Qonaq* in Kazakh, meaning "guest";

Also in Chelyabinsk is Lake Kaldy – *Qaldy* in Kazakh, meaning "remnant";

Prior to 1935, the city of Kuibyshev in the Novosibirsk region was known as Kainsk – *Qaiyñ* in Kazakh, meaning "birch tree".

I have had to leave out many interesting facts or describe them only briefly. There are so many place names like these. There is clearly good reason for this, of that there is no doubt. There are too many examples for this to be a coincidence. This means these are ancestral Kazakh lands that belonged to the Kazakhs in ancient times. The Kazakhs are their true owners. Vladimir Putin frequently repeats that Russia will never give up a single square foot of land. Well, no one wants to give up their native land, do they? We don't need other people's, and we won't let anyone take what belongs to us. The big question is: how did these Kazakh lands became Russian?

---

Prince Alexander Nevsky (13 May 1221 – 14 November 1263) had Kazakh roots. His grandmother came from the Kipchak tribe. Consequently, Prince Nevsky was directly related to the Kazakhs.

According to history, in 1240 Alexander Nevsky "advanced to the Neva with his band of men from Novgorod and Ladoga, taking the Swedish knights by surprise, and inflicted a crushing defeat on them." After this victory he was known as a hero. The people of Novgorod later "showed him the way out of the city", but in 1241 he was once more appointed Prince of Novgorod.

This is a new rewriting of history. What actually happened was quite different: the Swedish knights were defeated by Kipchak warriors on horseback. It was also the Kipchaks who facilitated Alexander Nevsky's return to Novgorod.

---

On many occasions I've had the experience of hearing Russia refer to other countries as aggressors. Let us remember our history here and recall what the territory of Russia was like six or seven centuries ago. There was no Russia, just some isolated principalities occupying small areas of land. What is Russia like now? Russia has amassed vast territories around itself, "continually trying to take over". And after all that, Russia is apparently not an aggressor? So many ethnic groups who previously inhabited these regions have vanished. Russia has incorporated these people's lands into its federation. It regards itself as an empire that has "no colonies". The "no colonies" claim is a misconception. It must have slipped their attention that all through the Soviet era it was totally obvious that all of the Union republics were subordinate to, and colonies of, Russia. Even today, all of the entities incorporated within the Federation can be called Russian colonies. Is there any sense in which the Chukchi, say, and the Northern peoples are not slaves? Or is Russian colonialism called something else?

---

Not long ago, in November 2016, at an awards ceremony at the Russian Geographical Society, the Russian president asked a nine-year-old schoolboy where Russia's borders ended. The boy answered, "At the Bering Strait", and Putin corrected him: "Russia's borders don't end anywhere." The way he said it set off alarm bells for me, and all of a sudden, Putin's prestige and reputation were shaken. Why did he put this question to a schoolboy and not to other world leaders, such as Xi Jinping, general secretary of the Chinese Communist Party? Or perhaps the question concealed a provocative ruse, and Putin had decided to intimidate others by proclaiming Russia's might and genuine threat to all?

Once upon a time, in sixteenth-century France, there lived an apothecary by the name of Michel de Nostredame (Nostradamus), who became famous for his prophecies. He "was worthy of recording future world events with his almost divine pen, thanks to the influence of the stars." One of his predictions, concerning the coming of three Antichrists, has given rise to a multitude of interpretations. The emergence of the following Antichrists is closer to the truth:
The first was Napoleon, who killed over 3.5 million people;
The second was Hitler. He was certainly a murderer and killer who was "born on the cusp of the ages". The second Antichrist "was predicted to emerge in central Europe". But in my view, this refers to Stalin, who "will lift up his wings so high in great power and might... there will be great strife, the blood of

innocents will be abundantly shed... as he attempts to seize lands." Stalin believed in nothing; he opposed religion, he murdered clergy or sent them to camps, he demolished Orthodox and other churches, mosques, Buddhist monasteries, synagogues and other places of worship, and he destroyed the sacred scriptures of the Bible, the Koran and the Torah;

The coming of the third Antichrist "shall be accompanied by wars"; "all kingdoms shall tremble with fear". He "shall destroy everything, even that which had previously been acquired...", "almost the whole world will be destroyed and laid waste", "a political crisis will erupt that threatens total collapse". This is presumably Stalin's successor: "driven by the imperial ambitions of his people, he shall restore his power over the whole territory by force of arms." And Russia is where we should look for him.


12.

Many languages are spoken around the world. It's very difficult, and indeed wrong, to single out or give preference to any one particular language: every language is beautiful in its own way. But since this book is about my people, the Kazakhs, I will now turn to the subject of our language.

According to our parents, the myth of the poverty and sparseness of the Kazakh language has been perpetuated in public opinion for centuries. The strange thing is that this myth has persisted to this day. I totally disagree with it. On the contrary, Kazakh is a rich and multifaceted language, centuries-old yet still under-explored. Kazakh vocabulary is enriched with many gradations of respectful address. Affixes and suffixes can be added to give affectionate undertones to the polite form of address. For example, *äketai* (äke – father), *anajan* (ana – mother), *künim* (kün – day, sun), *şyraǧym* (şyrak – candle), *aǧataiym* (aǧa – elder brother).

Kazakh also has some fascinating and rather odd turns of phrase that you imbue with emotion when you say them, but if you try to translate them literally, the feelings are not the same, because they are perceived and interpreted differently and sometimes sound comical, or even offensive. For this reason, such collocations are often paraphrased. Here are a few such turns of phrase:

*köziñnen ainalaiyn* – literally "I will whirl around your eyes" – means "beautiful, beloved";

*ayaq astynan* – literally "from under my feet" – means "unexpectedly";

*mūrnyna su jetpei* – literally "not enough water in my nose" – means "to be very busy";

*mūrttai ūşyp* – literally "to fly like a moustache" – means "to be very tired";

*ayağy auyr* – literally "heavy foot" – means "pregnant".

The Kazakhs typically choose meaningful baby names reflecting the time and place of birth, the baby's sex and other factors (Aisūlu – moon beauty, Künsūlu – sun beauty) and richly descriptive place names (River Aqsu – white water, Jezqazğan – they dug copper). Each season comes with its own verb – winter has arrived (*qys keldi*), spring has been born (*köktem tudy*), summer has come out (*jaz şyqty*), and autumn has fallen (*küz tüsti*).
Similar details are found in practically every aspect of life – festivals, meals, life stages, and so on. They are subtle, distinctive, insightful, and mindful of traditions and culture.

And yet Stalin planned to wipe the Kazakh people and their rich language off the face of the earth. His crimes were of a magnitude that had never been seen before. Who will hold this tyrant to account for them?

A good few of our parents' stories concerned not only the richness of the Kazakh language, but also the wealth of Kazakh art and culture, its inexhaustible heritage of classical poetry and music – a treasure-trove of thoughts and ideas. We have a veritable goldmine of proverbs and sayings, folktales, songs, epics, jokes and catchphrases applicable to every situation in life. In their wide-ranging songs, Kazakh improvisational poets (*akyns*) would celebrate the richness and beauty of our language, history and traditions. They conveyed the music of the boundless expanses, feather-grassed steppes, scorching hot deserts, inaccessible snowy mountain peaks, and smooth, clear blue rivers and lakes. The Kazakhs healed by playing their ancient traditional instruments – the *dombra* and the *kobyz*[20]. The sound of folk tunes would conjure up an image of the open steppe, its grass ruffled by the wind, and a dashing and intrepid rider flying past on his high-spirited winged steed. Instrumental pieces (*kui*) played on the *dombra* produce enchanting melodies; they sing of love and life, radiate joy, light and inspiration, banish fatigue, revive suffering souls, and fill you with spiritual peace and calm. They combine such feeling, such lyrical poetry, such spellbinding colours and shades that send shivers down your spine and take you flying heavenwards to the clouds. The smoothly flowing music of Kazakh waltzes goes straight to the heart; it is healing, captivating, and reveals a secret magic. The melody caresses the ear with such gentleness and sweetness, it brings out the love and springtime in our hearts, and stays with us. Kazakh writers, composers and artists create masterpieces that have been universally acclaimed.

Here is how Yermek Serkebayev, a Kazakh-Soviet chamber and opera singer and People's Artist of the USSR (4 July 1926-16 November 2013), described Kazakh music: "I've never had a problem saying that Kazakh melodies and Kazakh themes are just as beautiful as Italian musical themes. We have such beautiful and complex singing. Yet some Kazakh without any education wrote these songs – it's like a miracle! With the richness of the Kazakh language, the music is rich too."

Improvisational poetry duels (*aitys*) are popular among the Kazakhs. The participants banter with each other in a freeform sung dialogue on random subjects, addressing current real-life issues. A distinctive feature of these contests is that the song lyrics are thought up on the fly: the poems are composed ad lib – anything goes. An *aitys* demonstrates the expressiveness, singing tone and rich folklore of the Kazakh language.

---

[20] Stringed musical instruments: the *dombra* is plucked, while the *kobyz* is played with a bow. *(Translator's note.)*

Improvisation duels are part of the unique cultural legacy of the Kazakh people – the genre of oral folklore. The roots of the *aitys* are deep indeed, resting on many centuries of tradition.

As the *akyns* deftly pick at the *dombra* strings, they show off their skills of wit, resourcefulness and virtuoso acting. They talk in riddles, non-stop, full of emotion, eloquence and allusion. Embedded in their poetry are special subtleties and hidden meanings which are impossible to translate exactly without losing their sense or sparkle. But you can get by without a translation. All you will need is some knowledge of the language.

One Kazakh *akyn* poet, Zhambyl Zhabayev (February 1846-June 1945), was forced to write poems in praise of Stalin by the Soviet leadership. And he, a distinguished old man, said nothing out of turn. He was awarded a medal "For Valiant Labour in the Great Patriotic War 1941-45", the Badge of Honour, the Order of the Red Banner of Labour, the Order of Lenin, and the Stalin award, second class, for his well-known poetic works.

I'd just like to digress a little here and talk about some Kazakh *batyrs* (heroes), *akyns* and artists.

There have been so many wonderful folk singers: Yermek Serkebayev (the King of Baritones), Nurgali Nusipzhanov, Alibek Dnishev, the twin brothers Muslim and Rishat Abdullin, Roza Baglanova (Great Daughter of the Great Kazakh Steppe), Bibigul Tulegenova (the Kazakh Nightingale) and Madina Yeralieva. Their songs touch our souls and delight our ears with their beauty and clarity of voice.

Shamshi Kaldayakov is regarded as the king of the Kazakh waltz. He is a true *batyr* (hero) of the Kazakh people who lit up the stage in Kazakhstan. In 1956 he composed a ceremonial piece of music to inspire patriotic feelings; when Kazakhstan gained independence, it became the national anthem. In 1968 Kaldayakov spoke out against the handing over of Kazakh land to Russians.

Our greatest thinkers are Hodja Ahmed Yasawi, Al-Farabi and Abai Kunanbayev. Their philosophical treatises are the embodiment of our cultural heritage and keep our hearts and minds on the right track.

Shaken Aimanov was a multitalented Kazakh actor, theatre and film director and scriptwriter, a People's Artist of the USSR. The Kazakhfilm studio has been named after him.

I can't leave out Kazakh-Soviet poet and writer Mukhtar Shakhanov. It was he who spoke out in 1986 when Mikhail Gorbachev described the December events[21] in Kazakhstan as a demonstration by drunken youths. Shakhanov is also a true national hero.

Nothing is dearer to the people than independence. It is their great achievement and treasure. Our ancestors strived and fought for it for centuries, dreaming of unity and freedom. In July 1917, the Alash party was founded by some noted statesmen and politicians, crusaders for freedom and independence – Beimbet Mailin, Alikhan Bukeikhanov, Mustafa Shokay, Magjan Jumabayev, Akhmet Baitursynov and many others. The Alash party slogan – "Kazakhs, awake!" – vividly sums up its activity. They founded a national newspaper, *Qazaq*, which had "standing up for the ethnic name of the people" as one of its most important objectives.

Their freedom-loving ideas and desire for independence meant that the Alash Orda[22] leaders came to be regarded as enemies of the people. They were brutally executed by the Stalinist monsters.

We have so many great national heroes who are worthy of our esteem and respect. They were not afraid to go against the powers-that-be, they didn't back down, they defended their people to the end, devoting all their strength and even their lives to the struggle. That's real heroism; these are true national heroes. We bow our heads in respect to them and will cherish

---

[21] Protests that broke out in response to Gorbachev's seemingly arbitrary replacement of Dinmukhamed Kunayev, First Secretary of the Communist Party in Kazakhstan, with Gennady Kolbin, an unknown Party boss from Russia. *(Translator's note.)*

[22] The Kazakh provisional government, 1917-18. *(Translator's note.)*

their memory for ever! We remember them and deeply mourn them.

We have something unique that makes me proud and exultant: the free, unbounded steppe. It sees and understands everything, it keeps secrets, it has kept silent for centuries. Believe me, this is true. I hear how wonderfully the steppe sings, I see the high turquoise sky and the night's flickering starlight spilling out onto the snowy mountain tops. Wide-open expanses, boundless fields, scorching hot deserts. Rich subsoil resources, a bountiful land. Come and see for yourselves: you can walk through national parks and nature reserves, then relax and recuperate at resorts and spas with healing mud and mineral springs. You can see picturesque nature, extraordinary landscapes, indescribably beautiful mountains, pearly lakes, rivers and seas. You can hear how even the sands sing and smell the scent of the steppe that is like nowhere else. You can get to know Kazakh people and sample traditional Kazakh delicacies. And our steppe produces extraordinary people with generous, freedom-loving hearts. The Kazakhs are an incredible people with a unique ancient culture and a fidelity to their traditions and customs. As a people they are peaceful, non-aggressive, hospitable, friendly, musical and multi-dimensional, with their own festivals and rituals and a deep respect for their ancestors. It is part of Kazakh etiquette to treat everyone with politeness and courtesy, irrespective of their age and situation. A pure-blooded nation in which intra-clan relationships and marriages between members of the same ancestral group are strictly prohibited down to the seventh generation. The Kazakhs' most precious qualities are solidarity, help, support, tolerance, fellow feeling, mercy and compassion. Stalin knew all this. That is why he tried to crush these people who, by all the measures listed above, were better, nobler and purer than he was.

13.

I learned from my parents about the forced migration of ethnic minorities from every region of the USSR to the fertile Kazakh lands that had been vacated during the Holodomor. The

Kazakhs, having experienced the arbitrariness of Stalin's rule themselves, and having survived famine, economic ruin and the loss of loved ones, were understanding and friendly towards all of the immigrants. In the Kazakhs, the migrants found compassion, warmth and support.

The autumn of 1937 saw the deportation of Koreans from the Far East, Kurds, Azeris and Turks from the Caucasus, and Greeks, Jews and Poles from all over Russia. In late 1941 and early 1942, people were deported on flimsy political grounds from the Caucasus, Ukraine, the Baltic states, the Volga region and the Far East. Cold, hungry and often unwell, they were transported in filthy goods trucks meant for livestock. Labour camp prisoners were also transferred to Kazakhstan. In spite of the propaganda and misinformation being spread by the NKVD, claiming that the people from the Caucasus ate human flesh and that the Germans were fascists, people in the *auls* gave shelter to the exiles. Even though they themselves were struggling to survive, every Kazakh family reached out to any new arrivals, opened their doors and welcomed them into their homes without a second thought. They had not lost their consciences, their kind hearts, or their compassion. Nor were they put off by the fact that the migrants held different religious beliefs from them. When my parents were little, they saw how the migrants, gaunt and ragged, wolfed down their food. The Kazakhs had experienced more than enough sorrow, done more than enough wandering, and suffered plenty of hardship and violence, but it had not made them bitter. They did not turn their backs on others' suffering; they were ready to help the millions of people who had fallen on hard times, irrespective of their origins, family or tribe. Everyone in Kazakhstan did the same: they took in hundreds of deported families, gave them help and support, shared whatever they had – food, clothing, shelter – and helped them find work. No one stood aside, no one asked whether you were Kazakh or Russian, Ukrainian or Chechen, Bulgarian or German, Estonian or Polish, Korean or Jewish; that didn't matter to them. Friendship and sharing were part of their way of life. The children grew up together, played and studied all mixed up together. A single street would be home to Serikovs and

Shvetsovs, Kononenkos and Chentayevs, Dmitrovs and Richters, Tamms, Lees and Rifs, and many other families living together as neighbours.

The wrath and rage of Stalin the torturer knew no bounds. In February 1944 the Chechens and Ingush were driven out of their ancestral homes in the Caucasus on his orders. Their land, too, was coveted by Stalin. In May 1944, also on Stalin's orders, the Tatars were forcibly evicted from their ancestral lands in Crimea and loaded onto cattle trains. Russians were settled in the lands of the Crimean Tatars, the Volga region and Ukraine.

Officially, it was said at the time that the Tatars were being resettled in Central Asia and Kazakhstan. But this was a typical cunning ruse of Stalin's. In fact, they were not transported to Kazakhstan, because Stalin had heard that the Kazakhs had taken in and sheltered the previously deported Germans, Caucasians, Balts and Poles. Over 2 million Crimean Tatars were sent to Western Siberia. Thousands of NKVD operatives were drafted in to supervise the forced migrations. Many people died of malnutrition and disease on the journey. There was no medical care, and those who died were not permitted to be buried; their bodies were just thrown off the train. Whole families lost their lives. Stalin had accused the Crimean Tatars of collaborating with the Germans and forbade their return to their native land. In the late 1970s when we were university students in Tomsk, we rented a flat from some Tatars. They talked to us about Crimea, their historic homeland, and showed us photographs. They said how much they missed it and had not lost hope of returning one day.

The Tatars lived through a long and arduous period of repressions, struggle, deprivation, prisons and camps. The ban on their return endured until 1989. It was thanks to Raisa Gorbachev that Mikhail Gorbachev, as Chairman of the Supreme Soviet of the USSR, overturned the ban. Written sources record that in November 1989, the Supreme Soviet of the USSR declared the deportation of the Crimean Tatars to have been unlawful and criminal. Not that the term "deportation" should be applied to the Crimean Tatars, or to the

Chechens or Ingush either. Foreigners are deported for being on another state's territory without permission, whereas the Chechens, the Ingush and the Crimean Tatars had lived for centuries, indeed millennia, in the lands that belonged to them, from which they were forcibly evicted. The 1990s saw the Crimean Tatars begin to return to their historic homeland. Upon returning to Crimea, they once again purchased or built homes and found work. Not all of them were able to go back: some could not take the risk of losing the way of life they were accustomed to and building a new life from nothing.

Following the unlawful forced resettlement of the Crimean Tatars, the Bulgarians and Greeks were also deported from Crimea.

We did not witness the terrifying horrors of the past. We have been fortunate enough to live in a time of peace. When I was a schoolgirl, I would hear people of German, Lithuanian, Polish, Chechen and Ingush ethnicities, young and old alike, say that it was thanks to the Kazakhs that they survived. "The first people to offer us a helping hand and give us support were the Kazakhs. We remember all the good deeds that the Kazakh people did. They were cold and hungry themselves, but they did not leave us to starve and freeze to death. We cannot thank the Kazakhs enough. They helped Chechens, Germans, Ingush, Jews, Poles and others – anyone who needed help. Kazakhstan is sacred to us. We applaud and thank the whole Kazakh people for their kindness and their warm hearts" – these words of gratitude have been said many times over the years, and still are today.

In moving other ethnic groups onto Kazakh territory, Stalin had hoped that they would die of cold and starvation on the steppe, that the Kazakhs could not and would not help as they were still reeling from the Holodomor. But his plan failed.

And so the Balkars, Germans, Caucasians, Koreans and others ended up in Kazakhstan by the will of fate. They found shelter and a warm welcome, and here they remained. Kazakhstan

"became a home for those in need.

It taught its people how to live in peace,

And it was not afraid when times were tough,

Trusting its vision and strength would be enough."
The Kazakh steppes have brought together over one hundred different ethnic groups and faiths. The generous, hospitable Kazakh land became their homeland. Later on, they put down roots: they married Kazakh men and women, started families, and live here happily to this day, regarding Kazakhstan as their native land. All the peoples of Kazakhstan are united, and in that unity lies their strength and success. As Nursultan Nazarbayev, first president of Kazakhstan, said in his speech at the opening of the Monument to the Victims of the 1932-1933 Famine, "Despite all the hardships they faced, all those who were deported found a new life in Kazakhstan thanks to the hospitality of the Kazakh people. Today their descendants are our fellow citizens. Together we are building a strong and independent Kazakhstan as we journey towards peace and creativity!"

14.

In Kazakhstan we're allowed to study and communicate in whatever language we like; everyone is free to choose, regardless of ethnicity, situation and status. I have heard one high-ranking official from the Russian Federation insist that land belongs to the people whose language the inhabitants use to communicate. And former US president Donald Trump (who was president from 20 January 2017 to 20 January 2021) claimed that Crimea belongs to the Russians because according to him, everyone there speaks Russian.
This is complete rubbish, the product of a truly warped imagination! What are the implications of that interpretation? Kazakhstan isn't the only place where the majority of the population speaks Russian – this is also the case in other formerly fraternal republics of the Soviet Union. That's because we were all under the Russian yoke: ethnic language-medium schools were prohibited; the status of other languages was downgraded, and they were considered second class.
It's no secret that most of the ethnic Russians lived in large cities. And they were given flats – three or four per family. The indigenous population – the Kazakhs – weren't allowed to live

in the cities; you had to have a residence permit. However hard they tried, their efforts got them nowhere. Meanwhile, incoming Russians had no problem securing either housing or employment. There were six children in our family. My father was allocated a two-bedroom flat on a housing estate. Our Russian neighbours one floor down from us were also given a two-bedroom flat: their family consisted of a husband, wife and two children. In addition to this flat, when they registered their parents as living there, they were allocated another two-bedroom flat in the centre of town.

The Soviet policy on nationalities stated that "All ethnic groups and peoples shall be equal irrespective of where they live." The reality was very different. The USSR did not provide equal conditions for all its peoples. We may have lived in the same country, but the interests of individual ethnic groups were ignored, and the culture and traditions of other peoples were not respected. This begs the question: what about the foundation of spiritual life, spiritual fellowship and cultural unity? Alas, the authorities just weren't bothered about spiritual development.

In particular, despite the fact that the Kazakh Republic played a significant role in the overall development of the USSR as a whole and was a rich source of raw materials, the Kazakhs there were blatantly discriminated against, and their rights and contributions were diminished. As a result the Kazakhs, with all their principles, customs, culture and traditions, ended up with no voice in their own territory. They had no rights even within the boundaries that had been strictly delineated for them to live in – in their own republic. The government was stingy with finances. Funding to develop the Kazakh language, cultural heritage or historic traditions was only granted if there was any money left over.

In the capital, Almaty, it was not permitted to construct buildings that were architecturally superior to those in Moscow, or larger in size or capacity. The assumption was that Moscow always took precedence, and the best of everything should be concentrated there.

The Kazakhs didn't count for much in Soviet society. They carried little weight when it came to resolving intra-state issues.

For them, the route to prestigious jobs and positions of leadership was blocked. The Russians, as the dominant, privileged ethnic group, had a noticeably higher status than the others and benefited from special privileges. Only Russians could apply for posts of even the slightest significance; the Kazakhs' Russian language skills, level of education and years of experience would be disregarded. Nor could ordinary Kazakhs think of applying for more menial jobs such as janitor, night watchman, lift operator or cleaner, as these were normally drawn from the Russian population. Russians would not lose their jobs if they turned up drunk; they would receive their pay in full and keep their housing. Perhaps that was why they turned up their noses at us and strutted around as if they owned the place? Children from other ethnic groups would not get into sports clubs and teams; Russians were always picked first. When socialising, if there was just one Russian in a group of people, everyone would have to speak Russian. No Russian would ever have to make an effort to understand everyone else, yet everyone else had to make an effort so that the Russian could understand them. Ridiculous, wasn't it? But that's how it was and still is. Russians got the green light everywhere. The development of other languages was blocked. Preference was given to Russian, which was introduced to all the Soviet republics. Some schools had fictitious Kazakh lessons on the timetable that for various reasons were never properly taught. Learning about other languages and cultures was evidently considered pointless.

Even today, though the Soviet Union is long gone, the Russian language is still promoted, like it or not, in news outlets and TV shows from the Russian Federation, driving home the message that "knowing Russian makes you employable throughout the post-Soviet space". That said, note that "by law, foreign citizens who have entered and remain on the territory of the Russian Federation must pass tests of their knowledge of Russian as a second language, Russian history and basic Russian law… and those who wish to obtain a work permit must present a certificate confirming their knowledge of Russian as a second language." That's the set-up in Russia. There are no such tests, however, for Russian migrants seeking work in the neighbouring republics.

The result is a toxic ideology, a rabid Great Russian chauvinism[23], if they consider their ethnic group to be superior to and better than others. For them there are two types of people: Russians and everyone else. This sets a dangerous precedent and is creating an unacceptable situation. A toxic ideology is more powerful than drugs.

The Kazakhs were a minority in the cities. On many occasions I have heard name-calling, sneering and other taunts directed at Kazakh people. I do not understand why anyone would use such nasty, humiliating and contemptuous words that are not fit for human interaction. And in the Kazakh republic of all places! The name-calling would increase wherever the Russians were the majority. This produced a sense of psychological unease, as if you had ended up in a toxic environment and had no idea how to escape from it or what you could do to defend yourself. Who did they think they were (and still think they are)? It was total ignorance, lack of culture, addle-headedness. You don't big up one nation by doing down another. How can it be OK to judge people based on their appearance, dividing everyone into us and them? At the end of the day, it's not what's on the outside that counts – looks can be deceptive. The inside is what matters. Seemingly beautiful apples often turn out to have worms inside. I absolutely do not have a chauvinistic agenda. This sort of arrogance based on ethnicity crosses the line of what is acceptable. It does not sit right with me. Of course, everyone has their own perspective. From my point of view, the most important thing is to remain human, whatever the situation, and not lose our human face.

In the Soviet Union, and especially in Kazakhstan, Russian was considered the principal language. The state language was undermined; Kazakh was not the medium of education. In our city there were no Kazakh-language kindergartens, and there was just one Kazakh school, which was attended by children

---

[23] A term used by Lenin. *(Translator's note.)*

from outlying areas. My father sent us to a Russian-language kindergarten, then enrolled us in a Russian school, so that we would become totally proficient in Russian and be able to access a good education and make our own way in the world. Back then it was difficult, if not impossible, to get a decent job without knowing Russian.

For this reason, to my shame, I was totally ignorant of my own language: not only could I not speak Kazakh, I didn't even understand it. My ancestral language only became accessible to me much later, when I got married.

I have absolutely nothing negative to say about the Russian language.

A quotation from Herold Belger, a well-known Kazakhstani translator, prose writer, essayist and literary critic, seems appropriate here. Belger was born on 28 October 1934 in Engels, a city in the Saratov region of Russia, to a family of Volga Germans. Like all Germans in the USSR, he was deported to a Kazakh *aul* on the River Ishim in North Kazakhstan on Stalin's orders. He grew up there and acquired native-speaker fluency in Kazakh, attending a Kazakh-language secondary school and the Abai Kazakh Pedagogical University in Almaty. He spent his whole life, from his early years right up until his death on 7 February 2015, living and working in Kazakhstan. He embraced the Kazakh mentality, and his work explored Kazakh, German and Russian culture. He was the author, co-author, editor and compiler of a vast number of books.

This is what Herold Belger said: "I am passionate about and committed to calling for the revival and development of the Kazakh language. The Kazakh strings of my heart sing tirelessly of this…"

He also wrote, "I hope with all my heart that the natural might of the Kazakh language that has built up over the centuries will not melt or fade away or be lost on the steep and winding roads of centuries to come.

Multicultural Kazakhstan, and the long-suffering, ever-patient Kazakh people, and their unique and self-sufficient language, all deserve a great future, like its boundless open space."

I echo Mr Belger's words. I would just add that all other languages deserve a great future too.

I have the utmost respect for the people of all ethnicities who live on our planet. I don't divide people into us and them, as long as they come in peace. I have friends, acquaintances and even family members from different ethnic groups, and we all get on famously and understand one another.

"Treasure your native language – that is the moral credo of any person" – that's what Herold Belger believed. It's hard to argue with that. Everyone ought to treasure their native language, and everyone has the right to choose which language they wish to communicate in. I'm for honesty and integrity, peace and stability. I believe that peace is the universal desire of all peoples.

Be that as it may, the residue of this history remains. Clearly some people benefit from engineering conflict, stirring others up and egging them on, deepening the suspicions of those who already have doubts, adding fuel to the fire, and pitting people against each other. Some will follow their lead, parroting this nonsense and hyping it up even more. Then community relations are spoiled and hatred grows. There are too many predatory hate-mongers eating away at our society from the inside. Their less-than-clear consciences and their behaviour are devoid of morality. They give off a distinctly Cold War vibe. Slogans and soundbites from folks who are unhappy with the way things are generate nothing but negativity and aggression: they whip up tension, set the scene for societal fragmentation and internal collapse, change the mindset, sow the seeds of chauvinism, and inflame racial, inter-ethnic and religious hatred and division. There are various ways of describing this behaviour – Russian has a rich vocabulary. Let's go for a single pithy word that everyone understands: inhuman.

The world has become a harsh place to live in. It's only by coming together that we can help tackle the complex issues of community relations, turn down the heat and counter the hostile nationalist mood. We must tackle this seriously, thoroughly and peacefully, with wisdom and good judgement. People need a spiritual recharge.

In Kazakhstan there are no overt inter-ethnic conflicts or oppression. The Kazakhs are generous and hospitable by nature, just like the Kazakh land. The Kazakhs are a friendly people, easy to get along with.

One day, following our move from Kazakhstan's northern capital, Astana[24], to its southern one, Almaty, we were playing with our grandchildren in the children's playground in our courtyard. Some young Russian mums were sitting on benches a little way off. I'm not in the habit of encroaching on other people's personal space, and I don't like it when people focus on ethnicity, but here I will have to, because there is no reasonable explanation for what happened. Glancing in our direction, they expressed their displeasure in loud voices: "They come over here…" I'm at a loss to understand their problem here. Surely it's basic manners to respect the culture of the people whose land you live in? Our country has plenty of room for all of us if we welcome everyone heart and soul – no one is excluded. But some people are megalomaniacs, surly, unwelcoming and short on common sense, and they just want to stir up trouble. Mentally unstable people are susceptible to such provocations. If your religious sensibilities are offended, if you don't like something, you are free to leave. Why be so rude? *We* never accuse anyone of "coming over here", and it's our land! Basically, if you don't like it here, you can go somewhere where no one will offend you. I'd rather not have to think or talk about this, but if not now, when? I'm not writing these reminiscences to brag, but to record an event which actually took place. To send out a message to others so that no one else will want to do the same.

15.

The Stalinist diktat that anything to do with ethnic minorities must be annihilated did not apply solely to the Kazakhs. I want

---

[24] Renamed Nur-Sultan in 2019. *(Translator's note.)*

to highlight how the indigenous peoples of the North live in remote regions of the Russian Federation. They moved out of their *yarangas*[25] and into ramshackle, dilapidated old houses in a state of disrepair. It changed their way of life: their folk handicrafts, traditions and language were gradually forgotten. It was difficult for the reindeer herders to get to their camping areas. The village schools closed and there were no primary health care centres, let alone general hospitals. Children had to live apart from their parents, as they were educated at boarding schools. The standard of education may have been adequate, but there was no cultural development in the spirit of their ethnic traditions and customs, and no specialist teaching of their native language. The consequence of this interference in their customary way of life was desperately sad: these children barely knew their own language, had not been trained in hunting, trapping or fishing, and had lost the reindeer-herding and whaling skills they had acquired from their parents. Naturally, when they left school they did not return to their villages, where the socio-economic situation was dire: no opportunity to continue studying, get a good job, earn a decent wage, find housing, or provide for old age.

The Chukchi have lived in the tundra since time immemorial. For centuries they led a nomadic way of life, herding reindeer, hunting whales, walruses and seals, and fishing. By rights, therefore, these lands belong to them. The Russians rule the roost in these territories, exploiting the abundant natural subsoil resources. Having abandoned the nomadic way of life, the indigenous population has been left behind, subsisting on extremely low incomes. The Chukchi population is dwindling, while cases of cancer, tuberculosis and alcohol-related deaths are rising.

If the Russian government is unable to provide the indigenous population with jobs and decent living conditions, perhaps it would make more sense to take the Chukotka Autonomous Area

---

[25] *Yaranga* – a traditional tent-like mobile home made of reindeer skin. *(Translator's note.)*

out of the Federation and transfer these lands, together with the Northern peoples who live there, to be under the protection of the UN. We must save the Chukchi and other Northern peoples and revive their languages and cultures before it's too late. In this highly developed and civilised world, they too have the right to a life of dignity and freedom.

Stalin inflicted his reforms on the Kazakhs, and later the Ukrainians, unchecked, in pursuit of his objective of eradicating them. Outside the USSR, it seems, no one knew what was going on inside it. It was a miracle that these peoples survived.
Now, we cannot allow ethnic minorities to vanish, or for their languages to die out.
**The world has societies to protect historic heritage sites and endangered species of animals and birds. I'm calling for a society to be established to protect and support indigenous minority communities and preserve their languages.**

16.
Stalin never swerved from his path, pressing ahead with his villainous plans. He would fly into a furious rage if anything didn't go according to his plans. Their speedy implementation was thwarted by the German invasion.

People of every age and ethnicity from every corner of our immense Motherland rose up to fight in the holy war against the Nazis. Times were hard for everyone. The incalculable contribution that each of the peoples within our country made to victory must never be downplayed or forgotten. The Soviet republics supported the front as best they could: Azerbaijan, Kirghizia, Tajikistan, Turkmenistan and Uzbekistan sent oil, cotton and agricultural produce; Kazakhstan supplied grain, meat, clothing, lead, manganese, copper, iron and other metals. Nine out of ten bullets were made of lead from Kazakhstan.
The Panfilov division formed in Kazakhstan became famous for its part in the battles near Moscow. It prevented the Germans from taking Moscow in October-November 1941.

Not many Kazakhs went to fight in the war. This was because there was only a small number of Kazakhs left after Stalin's Holodomor. Nevertheless, on a per capita basis, more soldiers from Kazakhstan were awarded the title "Hero of the Soviet Union" than any of the other fourteen Union Republics. Among them were the celebrated women soldiers Aliya Moldagulova and Manshuk Mametova. And one of the soldiers who raised the red banner of Victory above the Reichstag on 30 April 1945 was a Kazakh, Rakhimzhan Koshkarbayev!

Rosa Baglanova, People's Artist of the USSR and Kazakhstan, performed on the frontline, lifting the seriously wounded soldiers' spirits with her incredible singing and her beautiful, inimitable voice.

Another heroine of World War II was the utterly fearless Khiuaz Dospanova. She was the only Kazakh woman pilot and was enrolled as a navigator. Bad weather and the risks of flying at low altitudes in a plywood night bomber did not stop Khiuaz from accomplishing her missions. Even after she was seriously wounded, she came back from the dead and returned to operations with both her legs smashed, enduring the pain with untold courage and strength of will. She was just outside Berlin when victory was declared. Dospanova was awarded the Order of the Red Star, Order of the Red Banner of Labour, Order of the Patriotic War first and second class, and other medals. But this legendary pilot never received the title of Hero of the Soviet Union as she so richly deserved.

Bauyrzhan Momyshuly began the war as a senior lieutenant in the Panfilov division. He fought in the defence of Moscow. He was put forward for the title of Hero of the Soviet Union eight times. There were other Kazakhs on the honour nomination list as well. But not all the nominations were approved by Stalin. In my view, this example of selectivity and rejection is further proof of his contempt for the Kazakhs.

---

Eventually the award found its way to the hero and Bauyrzhan Momyshuly's brave actions were given due recognition. Momyshuly received the award, though posthumously, in 1990 under Mikhail Gorbachev. His military tactics are now studied and employed by the Israeli army. Fidel Castro admired him, calling him a wise and legendary military commander. The Cuban leadership invited him to Liberty Island, where he was received with full honours.

As everyone knows, all decisions had to be run past the Kremlin. The great Kazakh composer Shamshi Kaldayakov was denied membership of the Union of Composers three times by Moscow, apparently because he had not attended a conservatory. Kaldayakov did not become a member of the Union of Composers until after his death, once Kazakhstan was independent. His rich creative legacy remains. He put his whole soul into his song compositions, where it lives on among the people.

---

There are many war heroes known and unknown, recognised and unrecognised. Lists of all those who were called up for active service from 1941 onwards have no doubt been preserved in the state Soviet archive. Unfortunately, not all of them lived to see victory. In any event, all of the victorious war heroes defended our common homeland loyally and well, irrespective of their ethnic origin. The price that the Soviet Union paid for victory was millions of human lives. Victory has no ethnicity, it is shared – hard-won by the blood and sweat of every Soviet citizen – and belongs not to selected individuals or groups, but to the whole Soviet people. And it will always remain one for all!

In 1991 the Soviet Union was broken up into separate sovereign states. One way or another, what we had in common will always remain common to us, and no one people has the right to claim our victory for itself. I would like the Russian state to remember this. Let's be clear about this. The people were united, and that is why no forces could crush them. They stood firm and overcame the enemy. And Victory Day, 9 May, is a day of remembrance – the most important Great Holiday.

17.
The role played by Kazakhstan in getting the economy going again was a significant one. Kazakhstan continued to hand over its grain, meat and other produce to the state. There was no let-up. Fired up with creative energy, the people never lost heart. They revived agriculture, developed light industry, and rebuilt villages, towns and cities. And yet it was in Kazakhstan, on 29 August 1949, that the Soviet atom bomb was first openly tested. Its yield was 22.4 kilotons – more powerful than Hiroshima or Nagasaki. Semipalatinsk was the fourth largest nuclear test site in the world in terms of destructive potential. Fourth in the whole world! It covered an area of 18,500 sq. km.

Little Boy, the atom bomb dropped by an American bomber on the Japanese city of Hiroshima on 6 August 1945, contained the equivalent of 13-18 kilotons of TNT. Up to 166,000 people lost their lives as a result.

Stalin was unperturbed by the suffering inflicted on Japan. The tragedy merely nudged him towards new trains of thought. He wasn't going to stand aside while America forged ahead; he wanted to have nuclear weapons like these himself.
"Two years later the Semipalatinsk test site, the future theatre of Soviet nuclear testing, emerged in the USSR."
In 1949 the Stalinist authorities crowed to the whole world: "… The USSR's military nuclear programme has yielded its first results: the first Soviet atom bomb, RDS-1, was detonated on 29 August 1949." Imagine the jubilation of Stalin and his cronies at the "successful blast".
Think, dear reader, really think about what the Soviet leaders were congratulating themselves on: what sort of programme, and what results. The result was murder. They were bragging about the creation of the "first Soviet atom bomb", but there was no mention of the specific location of that lethal test site, that it was in Kazakhstan, that people lived there, or that it hadn't even occurred to anyone to move those people, let alone the population of neighbouring areas, further away for safety reasons. Underground explosions continued to release deadly

radioactive fallout into the atmosphere. A vast territory far beyond the boundaries of the test site was heavily contaminated. According to published data, 456 nuclear tests were conducted at Semipalatinsk. The total yield of all the nuclear blasts before 1963 was equivalent to over 2,500 Hiroshima bombs. It's dreadful to imagine. That's enough destructive capacity to wipe out the whole human race…
That's the force of the blasts that we know about. But how many were there really?

Let's do some basic arithmetic. Even leaving out the fact that each explosion at the test site was many times more powerful than Hiroshima, if you multiply the number of those who died at Hiroshima by the number of blasts at the test site, you get an eight-digit number:
166,000 x 456 = 75,696,000.
Or another rough calculation, taking the total charge strength into account:
166,000 x 2,500 = 415,000,000.
Think, dear reader – not one life lost, not dozens, or hundreds, or thousands, but millions! And that's using the most basic calculations and a blast yield of up to 18 kilotons – but the blasts in Kazakhstan were super-powerful.
It's hard for me to write… tears are blurring my vision and choking my throat…

Years later Igor Kurchatov, father of the Soviet atomic bomb, acknowledged that he had invented a "terrible thing". But at the time, "in view of his exceptional contributions to the Soviet Motherland with respect to the application of nuclear energy", the "USSR Council of Ministers" ordered that Kurchatov be awarded "the title of Hero of Socialist Labour; the sum of 500,000 roubles (in addition to the previous payment of 50% of the award in the amount of 500,000 roubles and a ZIS-110 car); the Stalin Prize, first class; a detached house and a dacha, to be built and furnished at the state's expense; double his salary for the entire duration of his work in the field of nuclear energy; and the lifelong right (for both him and his wife) to free rail, boat and air travel within the USSR."

How can this be? Inventions that caused death and unimaginable suffering were regarded as exceptional contributions – and deserved to be so richly rewarded?

Kurchatov acquired a taste for state honours, rewards and privileges. Having built the atom bomb, he didn't stop there. He went on to direct the development of the USSR's first hydrogen bomb, with a yield of 400 kilotons. It was detonated on 12 August 1953 – once again at the Semipalatinsk test site. Is that anything to brag about? Thermonuclear weapons have an even greater potential explosion yield than nuclear weapons.

On 22 November 1955, a bomb was dropped that yielded 1.6 megatons of explosive force. According to the documentation, that was the most powerful device ever tested at the Semipalatinsk test site.

1955 saw the establishment of another test site in Kazakhstan – the Baikonur space launch facility in the Kzyl-Orda region, which has generated a greater quantity of harmful emissions than has been admitted. The next military testing ground, Sary-Shagan, was built in the Karaganda region in 1956 to develop and test missile defence systems.

Despite all of the benefits and privileges he was provided with, Kurchatov died at the age of 57, presumably as a result of his work handling deadly substances. But what about the people? The ordinary people who lived, and still live, in the vicinity of the test site where powerful explosions were directly caused by the deadly substances that he and other nuclear physicists had invented? Following the October 1963 ban on testing in the atmosphere, in outer space and under water, only underground blasts were officially documented, but in fact, ground and aerial explosions of tremendous force continued to be carried out. For over forty years the Kazakh land has shuddered from each new blast, while the testers have been lauded for their latest successful test. For millions of people, the testers' successes have resulted in premature deaths, miscarriages and babies born with deformities. The blasts have swept away millions of lives and have deprived millions more people of the chance of a normal life, ruining their health, inflicting deformities and disabilities on them, leaving them half-dead. These devastating changes have affected, and still do affect, other living creatures as well as human beings. The land, and the air, and the water all around the test site, and for thousands of kilometres beyond it, are contaminated. Everything has suffered from these lethal effects. How many times would the shock wave of all the bombs that have exploded at the test site have circled not just the whole of Kazakhstan, but the entire globe?

The figure that is always quoted for the number of people in Kazakhstan who were affected by nuclear testing is over 1.5 million. This doesn't add up. Think! How can it be only 1.5 million? The true number will never be admitted. What good would the brutal truth do anyway? It would not save my people from the tragic consequences of Soviet nuclear experiments. The damage has been handed down several generations. "An everlasting scar on Kazakhstan", "hellish pain, torment and screams into endless space".

Semipalatinsk testing site
An everlasting scar on Kazakhstan
27 years on

It's more than a scar – it's a festering wound that never heals over, the deeply-felt pain of the Kazakh people. Our reason is clouded by the unceasing, inhuman cries from the inhuman suffering and torment.

This is sobering in the extreme and I don't think it can leave anyone indifferent. How did it happen that Kazakhs defended Stalin's country during the Second World War, but could not defend their own country of Kazakhstan against the establishment of the lethal test site in 1949 and the testing of such powerful heavyweight thermonuclear devices? Did the people have no voice? My oppressed and subservient people…

There were many extensive, spacious areas within the Soviet Union. Why was Kazakh territory selected as the site for such a harmful testing ground? Surely other land could have been found for the deadly tests that would have been safer for people? Why did the Semipalatinsk test site "become a pet project of the ruthless arms race"? How did they dare to create – on our land – a hideous weapon capable of annihilating all living things?

In any event, the testers weren't satisfied with 400-kiloton blasts, and 1.6 megatons wasn't enough for them either. On 30 October 1961, a thermonuclear bomb with a record-breaking yield of 58.6 megatons was detonated at the nuclear test site on Novaya Zemlya Island. Tsar Bomba was "the most powerful explosive device ever created in human history". So it would seem that they *could* find somewhere uninhabited to test nuclear weapons. They could have built the site on that island and done all the tests there. Why was it necessary to bomb the territory of Kazakhstan? Why didn't they build that test site for their radiation experiments in the first place?

The answer is self-evident: because it was all part of the bloodthirsty genocidal policy being pursued by that brutal tyrant, Stalin. The Kazakh people continued to be used as guinea pigs, as did their language, culture, resources and territory. The Kazakhs had been selected as a target, and this triggered a chain reaction of horrific events and irreversible losses of life. The damage done is incalculable. The population has paid an appalling price for the testing of deadly weapons on Kazakh soil. This is the only nuclear test site in the world where, despite the terrifying research being done, the Soviet authorities did not give a thought to the people who lived there: they were not moved to safety, away from the contaminated zone with increased background radiation; not one village or town was closed. It's common knowledge that leaks of radioactive gases have caused irreparable damage to the people living there and the environment as a whole. Exposure to radiation has devastating and irreversible effects on the human body and causes serious genetic disorders. The repercussions of this massive radiation disaster will impact many generations to come. It's like a mine laid in Kazakhstan – a mine with a delayed and protracted effect.

Radiation from nuclear testing has contaminated the soil in most of the territory of Kazakhstan, yet the official estimate of the area affected is 304,000 sq. km. It will take at least one hundred years to clean up the land and get rid of all the hazardous radioactive waste.

All orders came from the Centre. Local people sent many petitions to Moscow requesting the closure of the nuclear test site and an end to the deadly experiments. But no straight answer or timely response to these petitions was ever forthcoming, and there was no reduction in either the number or the force of the blasts. Of course they couldn't have cared less, and still don't: after all, it isn't their land, and they can screw it all up and not give a damn. Kazakh writer, poet and activist Olzhas Suleimenov is the founder of a national patriotic movement. In 1973 he included the slogan "Long live the test ban!" in his poetry. These were the first protests against the test site. "For the sake of the health of present and future generations, for the sake of life on Earth, we demand the closure of the nuclear test sites!"

No public discussion of these matters was permitted. But in 1988, Rosa Baglanova, the great Kazakh singer and People's Artist of the USSR, summoned up the courage to speak out: "I went through the war. What's happening to the Aral Sea cannot be stopped with just words... We're talking here, but out there... nature is taking its course. What our – quote unquote – 'great scientists' have done... they are killing a whole nation in the womb... At any other time we would call this sabotage. But what are we supposed to call it if they are multi-award-winning academicians of the Soviet Union and Heroes of Socialist Labour ... Look at what we have in Kazakh territory: in Semipalatinsk, a nuclear test site; in Baikonur, a space launch facility; at the Aral Sea, a living hell... How can the Kazakhs keep going? If this was happening abroad, in America, we'd be shouting that they were killing the whole nation, not just in Kazakhstan… I have been to these places. I found it so hard. When babies are being born with no eyes… with no palate, without a hair on their heads, with no arms… no legs… What does this mean? Who should we be asking? Who should we be talking to? What level do we need to take this to for the pain and grief and the tragedy of the whole nation to be heard?"

That is the burning question that my people would like an answer to. They have been through so much agony and pain. How can those in power remain unmoved by their cries and fail to respond in any way? What has to happen for the authorities to wake up and get a reality check, for them to feel a stab in their hearts? How can we get the message across?
Nevada-Semipalatinsk, an anti-nuclear movement, was founded by Olzhas Suleimenov in February 1989. International by nature, the movement brought together victims of nuclear disasters from across the world. Its primary objective was a global ban on nuclear weapons. This was the first step back from the brink and towards general nuclear disarmament. Research at the test site continued until 1989. Nursultan Nazarbayev, the first president of Kazakhstan, signed the decree "On the Closure of the Semipalatinsk Nuclear Test Site" on 29 August 1991.
"The test site fell silent on 29 August 1991. But the darkened face of the Earth, its crevices and creases, clearly told the story of the site designed for death."
After the collapse of the USSR, the test sites were leased to Russia. Although the test sites were leased, their purpose did not change and the damage they caused did not diminish. The murderous experiments continued. After the latest launches in the programme, a Russian newsreader smiled as she announced the "successful testing of these beautiful deadly weapons". I cannot get my head around the idea that a lethal weapon could be beautiful. That newsreader is a woman, a mother, she has a son. How could she smile like that? Surely her heart was quailing and she was racked with anxiety at the thought of this terrifying success?

Why don't they build these space launch facilities and experimental test sites on their own land, in isolated areas away from the Russian population? Why don't they test their rockets and the rest of their nuclear arsenal in their own backyard, far away from Kazakhstan? The answer is the same – it's another attempt to cause harm to the Kazakhs. These experimenters are sick, and their sickness is a virulent plague that seeks to do away with the Kazakhs.

The Kazakh people have drained a cup brimming over with grief. So many lives have been cut short and destroyed…

Yet Moscow has remained unmoved by the boundless nationwide grief, profound sorrow and distress. "Moscow requested permission to conduct blasts that were laid in the ground. In exchange, it promised $6-9 billion dollars for regional development" (Sultan Kartoyev, vice president of the Nevada-Semipalatinsk movement).



Moscow seems to have lost the plot. They can't be right in the head. Can it really be that they don't care and they intend to continue the blasts, ignoring the grief of an entire people, and exchange human lives for regional development funding? Is that the price they put on Kazakh lives?

18.
Kazakhstan's whole history is soaked with the blood, sweat and tears of the Kazakh people. It was terrible to listen and realise that all this was not made up, it was no myth or legend, but the horrendous, heart-breaking, gut-wrenching truth. I was shaken by the horrific things I'd heard, haunted each night by nightmares in which I saw the children's never-ending crying and heard their heartrending groans of agony. It was hard, too, for our parents to immerse themselves in their memories and rewind the tapes of their lives. They shared them sparingly. They were reopening old wounds and it was acutely painful for them. Their reminiscences pierced our hearts too and burned into our consciousness. Be that as it may, we must never be silent about this.

Although I was born in a time of peace, long after the horrors of the Holodomor, the echo of those years resonates in my heart also. The famine took away the lives of millions of people – our family members, neighbours, compatriots. A lump rises in my throat, my heart is gripped with fear, and tears roll down my face.

Our parents believed that we need to know and never forget this truth, this blood-stained chapter in the history of our state, and remember the appalling tragedy of the years of Stalin's reign. Ignorance is unforgivable. We have to know, talk and write about it, and pass that knowledge down to the next generations so that they too will know, honour and remember. Sooner or later a time will come when the atrocities and brutality visited upon our people will be spoken of out loud, so that lessons can be learned and nothing like Stalin's bloodthirsty and criminal regime will be repeated in any country ever again. So that the Kazakh people, who have suffered so much, will never again go back to those dark years of hunger and cold, sickness and uncertainty, deceit and disappointment, subservience and destitution, open contempt, sarcastic mockery, silent mistrust and fastidious disdain. So that such horrendous tragedies will never happen again and no one else has to experience what our people had to go through.

This is why I have included these painful reminiscences from the tragic period of our history, the misfortunes, disasters, trials and tribulations of our ancestors, who were dispossessed and driven to despair.

As I write, all that is in me is cold, I can barely breathe, and my eyes are never dry for a moment. My tears are for what they endured, the unbearable spiritual anguish and burning frustration.

We are proud of our ancestors, who laid the foundation for a peaceful and happy future for their descendants; we cherish them and hold their memory sacred. Our hard-won lives rest on their shoulders. The tragic events that fell to the lot of the Kazakh people are receding into the past, but the memory of the appalling tragedy that shook the Kazakh people will never disappear. It lives on in the hearts of those now living and will live on in the hearts of successive generations. We pay tribute to all previous generations with immense gratitude and a profound and sincere respect.

I learned about the oppression and planned extermination of the minority peoples of Russia's Far North. They too were affected by the bloody Stalinist policy pursued in Soviet times. They were introduced to alcohol to make them dim-witted, not really thinking straight, so that they could be controlled. They used to be given crates of vodka, which they called "fire water", instead of their salaries. Being even half-drunk would cause them to lose their reason and feel totally invincible. Most Chukchi are fishermen, reindeer-herders and hunters. At the time of the Revolution, they numbered at least 3 million. Now it is difficult to arrive at a precise figure. After the war, and to this day, their salaries were paid in vodka. They have no chance of being saved. Many ethnic groups in the Far North have been wiped off the face of the earth. It will be for historians to determine how many Northern peoples there were before the Revolution and how many are left today.

Alcohol was also used to control people in Kazakhstan. In the shops, the shelves would be groaning under the weight of various beers, wines, vodkas, liqueurs, brandies and so on. The sale of alcohol was deliberate. It was a continuation of Stalin's policy to exterminate the Kazakh people. The aim of that policy was to weaken, suppress, eliminate and kill off the Kazakhs in various ways, as they were of no use. Alcohol was on sale from 8 am to midnight, while in Russia only one type of vodka, Russkaya or Pshenichnaya, was sold between 4 and 7 pm. The Kazakh people never took to drink, however, but continued to work hard, support their native land, and raise their families.

19.

While on the subject of Stalin, I can't leave out the fact that during the Second World War, soldiers going into battle would each be given 100 g of pure spirit to give them courage. The result was that after the war, many of the survivors could not get through a single day without their now habitual frontline 100 g. During an offensive, combatants did not have the right to turn back. Some of them were very young lads, straight from school and still wet behind the ears. They weren't given a moment to think, to get over their fear of impending death. Commissars armed with machine guns stood behind the main front line to stop anyone retreating. Those were Stalin's orders. Sons had to shoot fathers, brothers, friends. We don't know how many soldiers were killed by enemy fire and how many by their own. Captured soldiers were sometimes able to escape. They joined the army, fought with the partisans and lived to see victory. Yet when the war was over, they were tortured and given ten-year or even longer sentences for having been German prisoners of war. The only thing they were guilty of was being captured by the enemy while defending their motherland. By comparison, German prisoners were released in the 1950s and provided with everything they needed: housing, health care and pensions.

Stalin created a cult of personality. He manipulated people and subjugated them to his will. There were people who trembled before his greatness, blindly bowed down before him and praised him to the skies, calling him the father of the peoples, the most outstanding leader of all time. After his death these besotted individuals went around weeping and wailing, praying that he would come back to life, deluding themselves that if Stalin was still alive there would be order, the Soviet Union wouldn't have fallen apart and it would be way ahead of every other country in the world. Many Russian citizens dream of going back to the Soviet era. They don't think – or don't want to think – about the consequences, the new victims there would be.

How can we deny how things really were? Can we forget the harsh years of Stalin's tyrannical rule and his countless human victims and erase these tragic episodes from our country's history? We cannot allow any revival of or return to a Stalinist regime! I don't understand people like this. Maybe they were pretending because they were being forced to weep? Were they deaf and blind, impervious to subtle hints? Or were they hypnotised by him, in a state of oblivion? Perhaps for them, the harsher and more ruthless the ruler, the dearer he was to them? Maybe they admired Stalin's bullying, his despotism, and his resolutely Satanic personality? I can't believe they would really want to live such a miserable existence, in constant fear that one night the secret police might come for *them*, having to kiss portraits of him, crawl on all fours, endure hellish punishments, listen to threatening exhortations, pass along the conveyor belt of death? All of us will shuffle off this mortal coil one day. How will these Stalinist sycophants and toadies be able to look those who died because of Stalinism in the eye? Won't their consciences torment them for having betrayed the victims through their support for the Stalin era?

The NKVD spared no one: neither their own people, the Russians, nor Germans, nor Jews. To this day the Jews won't talk about this – why? Probably out of fear of Stalin and his bullies.

Soviet propaganda created an aura of sanctity around Stalin, and his inner circle idolised and lionised him. Stalin was absolutely not the father or leader of peoples. He was a murderer and their most dangerous foe. And he can never shake off the label of murderer and criminal. He is dogged by nasty rumours, an evil genius who did a deal with his conscience, using murderous methods to gain power. Consumed by envy and his desire to remake the world the way he wanted it, he cleared the way to absolute rule for himself with great cunning. He disposed of all his political opponents with ease by playing them off against each other – the perfect backdoor manoeuvre. Capitalising on his power, he clamped down on any pro-active measures not approved by him and anyone who stepped out of line.

After the Revolution Stalin brought back serfdom: people in the villages had no papers and received food for their work rather than wages.

With his firm grip on the levers of government, Stalin was able to create an entire empire, which he ruled over with a rod of iron. After he became leader, he chose his entourage with the utmost care; his henchmen underwent a selection process according to his requirements. He dictated his terms, he did not allow anyone to cross his red line, and he did not permit even the slightest misstep. Those who still dared to cross that line were threatened with imminent death, except for a few rare cases where twenty-five years' imprisonment in Siberia was substituted. In possession of unlimited power and authority, and with any human qualities atrophied, he brought everyone to heel and swept aside anyone disobedient or unreliable. To him nothing was sacred: he showed no mercy and cared for no one, not even friends and family. I don't think anyone cared for him or respected him either. He was irritable, neurotic and unstable; people were afraid of him. He had contradictory tendencies. He had no friends. As if someone who would betray his own people could have friends! Since he himself was a greedy liar hiding behind a mask, he thought everyone else was the same. Whatever he did was based on self-interest and he trusted no one; his soul was filled with hatred and bitterness. He would lose his temper and fly into rages, hissing, exploding if anyone dared to disagree or argue with him. He was a crazy, paranoid maniac, totally unpredictable, who cold-bloodedly killed any unwanted "vermin" with whom he disagreed. He was a virus that humanity had to be rid of for ever.

Stalin worshippers hype up his fantastic achievements. But can we call them achievements when they were built on human bones?

Stalin is credited with winning the Great Patriotic War. That is ridiculous. He led a dissolute life, drank heavily, and never once went to the front during the whole war. He never left the Kremlin because he was afraid of everything, even his own shadow. The only exception was in November 1943 when he secretly flew to Tehran for a conference. That was it. He ruled from his bunker, collected dirt on people he was suspicious about, and sent his "sheepdogs" to kill them on the basis of the false accusations made about them. The great victory was won by the Soviet people. It came at a cost – incredible human endeavour, deprivation and loss, and hard work on the battlefield and on the home front. Leadership was provided by Marshal Zhukov, Marshal Rokossovsky, General Panfilov and other commanding officers, not Stalin. The role played by our allies – the US, Britain and other countries – should not be underestimated. Without their help the war would have been lost. They sent food, clothing, military equipment and oil products. We have heard from our veteran heroes in Kazakhstan that the frost in 1941 was fierce – it cut through to the bone. The soldiers would have frozen in the trenches and starved to death if it hadn't been for help from the US. Later I read what Soviet military leader Georgy Zhukov had to say:

"People now say that our allies did nothing to help us, but it cannot be denied that without all the supplies that the Americans sent us, we could not have built up our own reserves and could not have gone on fighting. We had no explosives or gunpowder. There was no way of getting supplies of rifle cartridges. The Americans really helped us out with gunpowder and explosives, and they sent us a lot of sheet steel. How would we have been able to manufacture tanks that fast if the Americans hadn't provided steel? But now people make out that we had everything we needed and plenty of it. Without the American convoys we'd have had no supplies for our artillery."

But even the Great Patriotic War came as no surprise to Stalin. The perfidious attack was not inevitable. It came about as a result of a dispute or misunderstanding between politicians.

On 18 October 1938, Hitler sent Stalin a message wishing him a happy 60th birthday and proposing joint external cooperation. After the two powers had entered into a secret non-aggression pact, Hitler and Stalin began to think about annexing and partitioning Poland. If this plan was successful, they could then take over and divide up the whole of Europe.

The military incursions into Polish territory by German and Soviet troops on 1 September 1939 sparked the outbreak of the Second World War. Following the invasion of Eastern Poland, Stalin had 60,000 Poles and their families deported to Kazakhstan against their will. Here, too, Stalin's objective was the ethnic cleansing of Polish territory so that Russians could later settle there.

Stalin went back on his agreement with Hitler when he launched military operations against Finland without Hitler's consent and annexed part of its territory.

Right up until 22 June 1941 Stalin was sending grain and metal to Germany to placate Hitler, even though Soviet citizens were living from hand to mouth. But his servility got him nowhere. The friction between them eventually provided an indignant Hitler with an excuse for attacking the Soviet Union.

Estimates of the Soviet Union's demographic losses during the Great Patriotic War vary between 7 and 46 million people depending on the publication. The high death toll was the result of mistakes made by the commander-in-chief, Stalin, one of which was that so many clever, experienced and highly respected scientists, military leaders, generals and marshals had been shot or convicted and imprisoned prior to the war breaking out. The army was left without knowledgeable commanders and intelligent leaders, and they paid for that with soldiers' lives.

Even the Germans noticed that human life had no value for Stalin. The film *Bastards* depicts real-life events that happened at the front: orphaned boys, who had already received death sentences for the crimes they had committed, were recruited into a group of saboteurs to carry out a clandestine operation. No one was bothered about their fate. They were doomed anyway and death was inevitable, so they were deliberately sent behind enemy lines and into the line of fire. If they were killed, no one would go and look for them. Soviet intelligence has done its best here too. "Our employees have consulted the archives of the Russian Federal Security Service (FSB) and Kazakhstan's National Security Committee (KNB), and after studying the archive materials, their verdict was that no such schools for training juveniles as saboteurs… existed within the NKVD-NKGB system, nor were there any archive documents on the dropping of sabotage groups consisting of teenagers that were organised by the Soviet security agencies." However, while denying the existence of such schools in the USSR, they claim that "at that time it was primarily the Third Reich that trained adolescents as spies and saboteurs: the Abwehr[26] recruited and trained 'children with a criminal background and abandoned children aged between 8 and 14' to be deployed behind Soviet lines and in the occupied territory of the USSR. It has been confirmed that the archives of Russia's FSB contain documents relating to a German school for training adolescents as saboteurs… The fact that child saboteurs were used by the Germans has been confirmed by the historian Professor Boris Kovalyov, who refuted the existence of this practice in the USSR.

There is no shortage of real-life stories that were later found to be myths, "artistic fiction", and "the 'child saboteurs' and juvenile saboteur training schools shown in the film *Bastards* are entirely fictional."

Well, yes, obviously the USSR was as innocent as a lamb. Nothing like that was done, none of it existed, everyone else did that sort of thing, just not the Soviet Union, and besides there are no records of it happening. Obviously not. How could there be if Stalin had all the mess tidied up?

---

[26] The Abwehr was the military intelligence and counterintelligence agency of the German Empire, the Weimar Republic and the Third Reich.

How can they deny it? The film was adapted from a book by Vladimir Kunin: "the screenplay is based on real-life events from Kunin's biography". In Kazakhstan there was a "special school for 'child saboteurs' upstream from Medeo" that was later turned into the All-Union School for Mountain Training Instructors. The mountain infantry was trained at this school. A Kazakhstani veteran, Yury Tuyutyan, "while an inmate in a juvenile correctional facility, was recruited by an NKVD officer in early 1943 and sent to a school for young scouts near Vladivostok… It [the school] was located in the taiga… they were taught Chinese, radio communications, and how to use pistols, machine guns and hand grenades… they learned about reconnaissance, tactics and camouflage, and dug trenches."
No doubt there were similar schools in other locations, but history remains silent about them.


20.
After the stories I'd heard about Stalin's regime, I came to the conclusion that Stalin hated people. I grew up with the firm conviction that he was a filthy degenerate, and there should never be any return to his brutal rule, those dark days in our history. His name should be a byword for tyranny.
How can anyone side with Stalin, defend him on the grounds that he built factories and collectivised farms, and give him the credit for the Soviet Union's victory over Germany? That's all rubbish. If it hadn't been for power-hungry Stalin, there wouldn't have been a war at all. Hitler didn't need Russia – he needed Stalin.
How can anyone forget the innocent Kazakhs and Ukrainians who were slaughtered, the extermination of the Jews, the Holodomor and the deportation of the Volga Germans, the inhuman torture that went on in prisons, the people who were shot or sent to the Gulag? Their families were branded "Enemies of the People", stigmatised and marginalised. Fearing for their lives, their friends and family abandoned them and neighbours would turn away; they were universally shunned. The children of Enemies of the People were not accepted anywhere; every door to them was closed in terms of higher education and

employment. It wasn't out of animosity that people avoided them, but fear of being punished themselves. It tended to be at night that the latest Enemy of the People would be picked up. In those days influential leaders and people's representatives always had a suitcase packed and ready. Men in black overcoats would come for them in black cars. This was the disfigured face of the bloody Soviet regime: fabricated accusations with hideous consequences, mistrust, vicious denunciations, unspeakable atrocities, highly sophisticated harassment, inconceivable humiliation, brutal violence, arbitrary arrests, extrajudicial shootings, mutilated bodies, the convulsive screams of the dying, the muffled sobbing and keening of those driven mad by the loss of their loved ones.

After secondary school, I succeeded in getting a place at the institute where I wanted to study. Having passed the first term's exams, I was on my way home for the winter holidays. The other passengers in my compartment on the train were having a lively discussion about life. An elderly lady told us her story. She grew up in a large family in which she was the youngest child. In the 1930s, her elder brother was working as the chief engineer at a factory. In 1936, on the basis of a made-up denunciation, first the director of the factory was taken away, then her brother. He was declared to be a criminal. Three months later his wife was subjected to physical violence and sent to do hard labour in far-off Siberia. There she caught tuberculosis and died in terrible agony. The children had lost both parents.

How many more families like this are there, how many human tragedies? How many lifeless villages and unburied bodies? During those years, Stalin eliminated over 90% of the most forward-thinking intellectuals and military leaders, including academics, writers, poets, designers, engineers, architects.

He encouraged people to take sins they hadn't committed upon themselves. He threatened them with coercive measures and punishment for their families – little children and elderly parents. Not everyone could endure such hellish torture. Many ended their lives by suicide rather than live long enough to be executed.

Stalin is a state criminal. He is guilty of the deaths of millions of innocent people and complicit in all the tragedies of the Kazakh people.

How could it be within his power to decide people's fates and to bring about such carnage?

Who will take responsibility for the lives ruined by Stalin? Who will repent? Everyone receives the appropriate punishment for their transgressions. What punishment, then, do Stalin and his henchmen deserve for the evil they have done? There is no mercy for them. They should get what they deserve. How can their crimes go unpunished?

The harshest punishment for any person is a guilty conscience. But did Stalin have one? Perhaps it was gnawing away at him? He should be found guilty. He should be subject to harsh retribution for the sins he committed. Who will commit a just act of vengeance against him?

There is no doubt that Stalin is the devil incarnate, a non-entity. We call him a tyrant and a sadist. We label him and we curse him. He is the one who personally signed the terrible orders, published the vile decrees, and condemned people to death with a single stroke of his pen. Stalin is blamed for all the lawlessness – and rightly so. But meanwhile, were the people who were close to him looking the other way? They weren't just observers – they were directly involved in enforcing the verdicts. What should we call these opportunists? They can justly be called tyrants two or three times over. They got rid of anyone inconvenient and controlled people's fates at their discretion. Some try to make excuses for these murderers, saying that they were only doing their duty. What duty? To whom? I don't know what could have been going on in their heads. And to make excuses for them! How did these monsters live with themselves, how did they sleep? Where can one find out the names of Stalin's lapdogs? Where did they spring from? How could they look their children in the face? Did they tell their children the truth – that they were lapdogs and murderers – or did they make up nice stories? What did they teach their children, how did they bring them up? What about the descendants of Stalin and his executioners? Are they proud of having ancestors who murdered millions of innocent people? Do they boast about them, or do they carefully conceal their roots? Can they live normal lives knowing what their forefathers did? Yes, children are not responsible for the sins of their parents, but how do they live with that burden?

Stalin was a cruel oppressor, an exterminator of peoples. His egoism, cynicism and heartlessness are astonishing. His insane atrocities chill the soul. We do not have complete information about everything that went on during Stalin's arbitrary rule, since facts and accurate evidence were deliberately concealed. There were many deaths and losses that no one will ever be able to atone for. We deeply mourn those who perished in the Stalinist Holodomor, those who gave their lives during the Second World War, those who are no longer with us. Neither we nor anyone else will ever know the whole truth about those who were ground to death in Stalin's mill. When Stalin died, most people breathed a sigh of relief. The empire he created has collapsed. The age of dictatorship is over. But time will not erase Stalin's villainy. For political reasons, data is hard to come by and we don't have exhaustive, detailed information, but the traces left by his bloody crimes are everywhere. There was not a single Kazakh family who did not suffer from his tyranny. The victims, and the sheer scale of the 20th century's most brutal crimes and inhuman punitive attacks, will live on in the memory of the Kazakh people.

Whatever people think of Stalin, as the despot of the Soviet period he is unquestionably a key historical figure. He should not be expunged from history. The important thing is that this should never be allowed to happen again.

21.
The Holodomor was denied for many years. There were no truthful publications, and those that did exist, little known and little studied, were either hidden far away behind the "Top Secret" classification or completely destroyed. The careful

arithmetic only slips up here and there. That was how Soviet censorship was. There was no hiding from the watchful, unsleeping eye of state scrutiny. No one dared to breach the ban on talking about the Holodomor because they would be punished for any conversation about the famine; they were intimidated in every possible way. Any facts presented would be explained away as an attempt to stir up hatred for the USSR. So as not to undermine inter-ethnic unity, they said. How can you undermine what isn't there and never was? The Soviet Union was declared to be a free country where everyone had the same rights and responsibilities. The reality was completely different – far harsher and more troubling. The rights and responsibilities of those who lived in this free country were not at all the same for everyone. Whoever is in power, there will be time-servers looking out for themselves, fixing themselves up with a cushy job. For their own survival, they grovel and suck up to their bosses, hoping to be given some tasty morsel. They dance to the authorities' tune, exaggerating the highs and understating the lows, dividing people up according to the colour and shape of their eyes and the shape of their face and nose, instigating and spreading anti-propaganda and filthy lies, and arrogantly trampling all over genuine time-honoured human values. They despise the generally accepted moral code. These provocateurs all have the same modus operandi – ruining, destroying, playing people off against each other, trying to stir up trouble.

The first time I heard our parents tell of the horrendous suffering of the Kazakh people, I was profoundly shocked. I had never had any doubts about how things were. Our history lessons at school had presented these issues so differently. That made the realisation all the more horrifying.
Eyewitnesses of the Holodomor – people who saw at first hand the organised atrocities that went on – assert with one voice that the famine was on a massive scale.

We are now in the $21^{st}$ century. But the question of how many people died in the Holodomor still remains unanswered, and accurate information on the flagrant abuse of the Kazakh people is still being kept secret. Various different statistics crop up in journalistic publications.

Let's try and open our eyes. Even with the cutting-edge technology and highly trained staff we have today, a population census takes three years to carry out. The data obtained has to be processed. Back then, people were poorly educated and means of transportation were limited. Kazakhstan is vast, and its inhabitants were scattered across the steppe, mountains and villages. A rigorous census would not have been realistic. The statistics given in the 1926 census were plucked out of the air and are far from objective. That figure was probably 25-30% of the population. Those were years of war, revolution, and roaming bands of rapists, looters and murderers. There was no justice system. Stalin had given massacres the green light. Commanders and troops alike slaughtered people indiscriminately, beating, beheading and shooting; they skinned people alive, buried the wounded alive, and raped whoever they wanted – little girls as well as women. Nothing was off-limits for them. Anything not to their liking would be immediately destroyed.

According to the historian Kaidar Aldazhumanov, in November 1991 a commission was set up within the Supreme Soviet and charged with studying classified documents in the archives of the law enforcement and security agencies. At the time, the commission described the famine in the steppe as "an act of deliberate malice against the Kazakh ethnos", an "ethnocide". However, the researchers from the Russian Federation were reluctant to accept the Kazakhstani historians' conclusions.

"In 1992, a government commission set up by Nursultan Nazarbayev, President of Kazakhstan, resolved that the Kazakh famine should be considered genocide…

Towards the end of the 1990s, however, because there had been so little academic research and public investigations into the catastrophe, public interest in the famine began to wane in Kazakhstan. The reasons for this shift need to be further explored, but it might have been because officials were concerned that further investigation into the famine might cast a shadow over Kazakhstan's close relationship with Russia… Nazarbayev implied that public discussion of the famine might be renewed, but in a more limited way: 'When we reflect on history, we need to be very wise and not allow the topic to be politicised. The cause of the famine, deportations and widespread loss of life was the brutal policy of the Soviet regime.' He urged Kazakhs to remember what happened, but warned them of the dangers of 'politicising' the catastrophe, as in Ukraine, where the Ukrainians are demanding compensation from Russia for the harm caused by their famine."

Since 1997, 31 May has been marked as the Day of Remembrance for the Victims of Political Repressions in Kazakhstan.

On this day, in various years, monuments honouring the victims of the tragic events of the 20th century have been declared open in different locations across Kazakhstan:

in 2002 a monument to the victims of political repressions was unveiled in the village of Zhanalyk, Almaty region;

in 2007 a museum and memorial honouring the victims of political repressions and totalitarianism was opened on the territory of ALZhIR, the former Akmola Camp for Wives of Traitors to the Motherland;

in 2012 a monument commemorating the victims of the Holodomor was unveiled in Astana;
in 2012 a monument to the victims of the Holodomor was unveiled in Pavlodar. It depicts a son weeping for his mother

who has died of starvation, with a broken *şañyraq*[27] in the background;

in 2017 a monument to the victims of the Holodomor was unveiled in Almaty: a sculpture of a mother holding her starving child in her arms. The words of Nursultan Nazarbayev, first President of Kazakhstan, are engraved on the base in Russian,

---

[27] *Şañyraq* – the upper dome-like portion of a yurt, symbolising peace and family well-being. *(Translator's note.)*

Kazakh and English: "The famine that pushed an entire nation to the brink of extinction will never be forgotten";

in 2018 – a memorial to the victims of the famine and political repressions was unveiled in Aktobe. It consists of a sculpture of an emaciated, barefoot person, shackled with iron chains, and two granite walls engraved with words commemorating the victims and a quotation in Kazakh from First President of Kazakhstan Nursultan Nazarbayev. Translated into English, the quotation says, "This tragic chapter in our history, and the victims of the political repressions and the famine, will always remain in our memory, and it is our sacred duty not to forget them." The granite walls are topped with a *şañyraq* – symbol of hearth and home;

in December 2018 – a Museum in Memory of the Victims of the "Red Terror" was opened in the village of Zhanalyk in the Almaty region. Together with the monument, it forms a single memorial complex.

Monuments and memorials dedicated to the tragic events have been built in other towns and cities too. There are over sixty in Kazakhstan.

These memorial complexes are a lasting commemoration of this dark chapter in our history, a silent reminder of the victims of this bloody period of forced collectivisation, repressions, famine and deportation. They are a symbol of our compatriots' unbending will, courage and patriotism.

Holodomor Remembrance Day in Ukraine takes place on the fourth Saturday of November. On this day of mourning, people all over Ukraine light candles and bring them to the monuments honouring the victims of the Holodomor.

Every year on 31 May, memorial events are held at monuments all over Kazakhstan. People come to remember and honour the memory of the millions of innocent victims of the political repressions and famine. No one and nothing is forgotten! Pain without measure, eternal grief…

22.

In 2000–2010, a group of western experts investigated the Holodomor with a view to determining whether it should be recognised as a genocide. They were Isabelle Ohayon of France, Niccolò Pianciola of Italy, Robert Kindler of Germany, and Sarah Cameron and Matthew Payne from the US. It would be interesting to know which data the investigation was based on, since after all, all data was painstakingly falsified under Stalin. Only one of these five academics, Matthew Payne, recognised the famine as a genocide. Perhaps the blood of those who deny it is the same that flowed in Stalin, Goloshchyokin and their ilk? Maybe they work in collaboration with similarly duplicitous, greedy people and are afraid of being misunderstood? How many people do they think, hand on heart, should have died for the famine to be recognised as a genocide? Surely there was no ban on them? When one person dies for no reason, we feel sorry. The death of just one person is a tangible loss. What, then, should we call what happened to the Kazakh people, millions of whom were killed by punitive measures, violence, massacres, starvation, cold, and yearning for their homeland? What can such losses be compared with? Is that not enough for the commission? Do they have no heart, no human soul? What, then, do they think genocide is? Is it possible to heal souls, to cure the wounds inflicted by the bloody Stalinist regime?

Ukraine has raised the issue of the Holodomor.
"It was only when Ukraine raised this issue at UN level that Russia began to say that 'The famine was not just in Ukraine, it also affected the North Caucasus, the Volga region, Mordovia, Kazakhstan and even the southern areas of Kyrgyzstan.' In this way they wanted to downplay the significance of the tragedy in Kazakhstan and Ukraine", wrote Kazakhstani historian Kaidar Aldazhumanov.
Yes, the famine did affect other regions of the former Soviet Union. But by asserting that people died of starvation in many parts of the USSR, Russia is avoiding giving a straight answer, omitting to say that Ukraine and Kazakhstan suffered the most, and that this was a deliberate bloodthirsty policy on Stalin's

part. How long will they hold their tongue and obstinately remain silent? The time has come to tell the whole world. Covering up historical truth only proves that Russia is weak and suggests that as long as the leadership includes people who are complicit in this, the truth will not come out.

The Ukrainian Holodomor of 1932-33 has been officially recognised as an act of genocide by over 20 countries around the world. A 2008 resolution of the European Parliament called the Holodomor "an appalling crime against the people of Ukraine, and against humanity". Russia's State Duma has refused to recognise it as a genocide: "This tragedy does not and cannot possess the internationally established attributes of genocide and should not be the subject of contemporary political speculation."

On 25 November 2017, at the monument to Holodomor victims in Kyiv, former Ukrainian President Petro Poroshenko (who was president from 7 June 2014 to 20 May 2019) "called on Russia to recognise the Holodomor, which took the lives of millions of people in Ukraine under the Soviet dictator Joseph Stalin, as a genocide 'or at least repent for it'."

"Historic responsibility for the Holodomor lies with the Russian Federation, as the legal successor to the USSR, and this crime has no statute of limitations", Poroshenko believes.

The Kazakh people has been through an incomparable tragedy. But even after that, "Kazakhstan's leadership continues to act with a careful eye on Russia". "Astana has not yet given a political assessment of the Famine."

"There is a major political factor underlying this issue: how to avoid offending our strategic neighbour, Russia. If we actually declare the famine to have been an act of genocide committed against the Kazakh people, then someone must have been responsible for that genocide. The Soviet Union at that time was responsible. Russia named itself as the legal successor to the Soviet Union, inheriting all of its overseas assets. In that case, the sole party responsible for the genocide carried out on the Kazakh steppes in the 1930s must be Russia. Because of our fear that this would damage or end relations with Russia, we cannot cross the line within our own psychology, and we are hesitant to speak out." That is the assessment given by historian Dosaly Salkynbek.

Perhaps it's time our leadership woke up and followed Ukraine's example by moving the issue forward again? "It's frustrating that despite the huge number of people who died in the famine, our government still remains silent." What are they afraid of? Why don't they understand? Those who perpetrated the deliberate act of genocide against the Kazakhs are no longer with us; no one is going to take revenge; there will be no new victims. This is not about vengeance and retribution. It's about stating what happened. 'Ukrainian historians… take the view that the famine in Kazakhstan should be regarded as genocide.' The time has come for our government to raise this issue on an international level and to set up a commission to reopen the investigation into the previous century's crimes against the Kazakh people while there are still witnesses to those terrible days left alive. The time has come to confront the truth and expose the crimes of the Stalinist regime. How long can we close our eyes and cover up for the criminals of the Soviet era, filling our heads with eulogies? It's time to stop glossing over the Soviet Union's flaws and only ever talking about its achievements.

The Ukrainian authorities were not afraid to raise this issue… Many countries have recognised the Holodomor as a genocide. We also need to tell the international community about the tragedy that took away the lives… of millions of Kazakhs… This would be an expression of spiritual renewal."

We are not accusing anyone or urging anyone to move against other ethnic groups. We are not raising the "question of the Soviet authorities' responsibility for the crimes of the 1920s and 30s in Kazakhstan", even though "documents that were classified as 'Top Secret' at the time contain the full names of Soviet decision-makers, from Stalin downwards." These crimes were committed by Stalin's bloodthirsty regime. Historical amnesia is a manifestation of ignorance. International recognition of the Holodomor as a genocide is not a tool for inflaming inter-ethnic hatred. However long it has been neglected, we must acknowledge what happened in the past and see that justice is done!

The Kazakh people have suffered so much. Not everything that happened has been covered by the media; some events have been lost in the current of history. But surely there has been more than enough tragedy! What more do the people have to suffer for the government to wake up and take some action?

Herold Belger, the German Kazakhstani I mentioned earlier, said something that I think fits perfectly here. "In some ways the Kazakhs' long-suffering, loyal nature is a good thing. A Kazakh can endure anything. But hunger, misery and being rounded up like cattle are not things that should be endured. Sometimes you need to get angry. As my friend the writer Alexei Debolsky used to say, 'You need to raise your hackles!' You have to take a stand, you have to disagree – to look them in the eye and say, *"Ai! Mynauyn ittık koi!"*[28] No, there isn't any of that."

At the end of the day, it doesn't matter whether the world recognises the Kazakh Holodomor as a genocide. That won't change much. What is important is that our government recognise it. It's time to stop shrouding these events of nearly a century ago in secrecy. It was a tragedy, what happened will never be erased from folk memory, and millions of lives lost can never be got back. No one will ever be able to state the exact number of all the victims. Whatever that number was, the victims can never be replaced. Their memory will remain in our hearts for ever down the generations. Despite the hammer blows it has received from fate, the spirit of the Kazakh people will not be broken. *Qazaq – myn olıp, myn tırılgen halyk!* (Translated literally: The Kazakh people a thousand times has died, a thousand times has risen!)

23.

All this happened long ago. I did not witness it. I know about it from my parents' eyewitness accounts and those of my husband's parents, and from the documentaries I've watched. Immersing myself in all that they heard and saw, and writing it

---

[28] "That's swinishness!"

all down, has been very hard. The subject is vast, and fitting everything in is inconceivable. Written reminiscences do not claim to be complete, and perhaps will never meet the designated standards of completeness; there are so many more secrets from that time that are unknown to us. But these long-ago events really did happen as I have described them. There's no getting away from that. I have written with tears rolling down my cheeks; I have written so that I myself will never forget, and so that others will know our history and the names of some truly great Kazakhs, and will know what sort of people our ancestors were and what they went through. "We need to learn lessons not just from victories and triumphs, but also from the painful events in our history. This is a warning not to let it happen again", says award-winning Kazakh historian Professor Kadyrzhan Abuyev. It's time to lift up the curtain, break through the information blackout and open up a wide-ranging public conversation. To be open about the past. All that was kept secret is being revealed. However devious the werewolves were, their day of reckoning will come.

Punishing the perpetrators and calling them to account might not be possible; they are no longer alive. But people need to know about them so that individuals like Stalin will never again be allowed to rise to power and commit crimes like his.

It isn't right to interfere in the lives of other ethnic groups, make them live under draconian laws and remake everything to suit you. This is a deeply personal, deeply individual matter for each country. People have the right to live in freedom in their own land according to their country's laws.
I don't understand why Russia has undertaken to involve itself in other countries' domestic affairs and why everyone has to submit to Russian influence, when Russia doesn't listen to anyone else and ignores other countries' interests. They say one thing, talking a good game for all the world to hear, and do something quite different. They can smile to your face, but behind your back they twist everything and say goodness knows what. Their own snouts are well into the trough, but they

eloquently cite and comment on everything that other countries' governments are doing, not missing a thing. They love to get attention, to "stir up public opinion", to create media hype. They're still using the Soviet slogan "Catch up and overtake!" today. They compare the West with themselves, railing against its "direct interference in our country's business". Well, what on earth do they think *they* do? Their long arms and long noses that poke in everywhere are forgotten. They accuse and condemn others without taking a look at themselves. There's no logic to it…

If some unbiased, unpalatable truth about Russia leaks out in foreign media, they are annoyed and indignant. Meanwhile they themselves denigrate others and get away with it. If they don't accept any criticism of themselves and don't tolerate others making nasty comments about them, why do they indulge in "constant mudslinging and muckraking" themselves? If you want others to treat you fairly, start by being fair yourself. Isn't that right?

The English word "fake" has now come into common use in Russian, meaning "fake news". Former US president Donald Trump used to deny any information concerning him, without troubling to go into the details, by calling it fake news. Journalists often describe any published item about Russia as fake news. The meaning of the word "fake" has done a 180-degree turn for me since Trump. When I hear "fake news", I assume the reverse.


Belarus, Russia and Ukraine refer to themselves as sisters. They belong to the same ethno-linguistic group – the East Slavs. In 1975 the "Three Sisters" friendship monument was erected at the point where the borders of the three republics intersect. The sisters who share a common past "look to the future in their different ways".

Russia does not want to accept reality. It dared to encroach on the territorial integrity of its sister, Ukraine, even preparing to send troops in. Yet the Russian bigwigs claim that "Russia never interferes". And after all that, "Russia insists that the annexation procedure complied with international law". How did they have the nerve to hold a referendum and seize Crimea – territory that belongs to Ukraine? Is that how sisters behave? The indigenous population of Crimea, the Tatars, were evicted by Stalin out of spite. Only for Crimea to be so dishonourably stolen by referendum decades later?

A presenter on one Russian political talk show declared, "The fact is that we're fed up with you going on about your Ukrainian language." So apparently, in her opinion, everyone has to speak Russian all the time, no matter what country they live in, and Russian has to take priority? I'd like to know why Russian is so privileged, in what way it's better. How can it be right to elevate one's own language and diminish others so publicly?

Why, too, has there been a policy of Russification for centuries, so that no one could get anywhere without knowing Russian? Why do they try to drum it into everyone, treating other languages as if they're nothing? Everything is supposed to be civilised. Why there is such a contemptuous and disparaging attitude towards other languages in the post-Soviet space, I am at a loss to understand. And what about moral attitudes, the conscience that underpins ethics, the rules that govern social behaviour? For me, every country has the right to freely choose how its people live their lives and which language they use to communicate. It seems I'm wrong about that?..

The world is being transformed through TV shows: all that is beautiful is disappearing; the old signposts that used to mark our way are being lost; moral principles and values are being washed away; the boundaries are being erased between good and evil, conscience and shame.

Russian journalists and presenters on state TV channels rely on a key phrase: "We show you the world as it is; we know what we're talking about." They manipulate public opinion and peddle propaganda, constantly emphasising in their programmes that "words have meaning". In order not to contradict themselves, they are doubly obliged, within the bounds of propriety, to watch what they say, be careful how they respond, keep strong negative emotions in check and not express them out loud. They lack balance and mutual respect, and they preach national supremacy, which is totally unacceptable. Their TV shows are corrupting society on a massive scale. How can it be permissible to mingle politics with your personal biases, or to discuss things like "Is she is stupid or only pretending?", "the new elite and the old" or someone's "unattractive" appearance, and to focus on "how hypocritical they are in the West"? Do these presenters have rubbish heaps for brains? Instead of looking at other people, perhaps they should think back to the fable about the mirror…?[29]

And what's going on in Belarus? This is another example of Russia's behaviour towards her so-called sisters. Russia should know better than to go to war against a neighbour. Or do they not have any brains in their heads to think with?

The ethnopolitical conflict between Azerbaijan and Armenia has deep historical roots. The conflict, which had died down for a time, has flared up again and entered a new phase. There have been periodic armed confrontations between the two ethnic groups. In autumn 2020 the tensions erupted with full force. There was mass civil unrest. Russian peacekeepers were brought in to deal with an incident. The deputy speaker of Azerbaijan's parliament expressed his displeasure at their actions, saying that "the new map they presented… goes beyond the agreement we signed." He said the Russian map "has no legal or political basis", since "it presents our ancient lands under other names." More division.

The Soviet government's policy of oppressing and harassing the Kazakh people in every possible way continues to this day. Following the annexation of Crimea from Ukraine, it's clear that Russia has set its sights on Kazakhstan. Russia's appetite for this became known among Russian students. This was demonstrated by a question put by a student at Peoples' Friendship University of Russia during the All-Russian Youth Forum in August 2014. She asked whether a Ukraine-type scenario should be expected in Kazakhstan.

---

[29] A well-known fable by Ivan Krylov in which a monkey looks in a mirror and refuses to recognise herself. *(Translator's note.)*

Vladimir Putin gave this astonishing response: "The Kazakhs never had their own statehood…"

This offensive statement by the Russian president is not unique. He has also said that "Ukraine did not exist" and "Georgia did not exist". Curiously enough.

The Russian regime is trying to distort history and smash a once-mighty system to smithereens. It disregards the fact that damage control, shoring up the foundation of a faltering system, is more complex: the system might break down completely. The Ukrainian political analyst Oleksandr Kochetkov has noted that "all through his reign, Putin and his entire neo-imperial machine don't just talk, they take practical action". By the look of it, they are trying to establish the "Russian World" ideology and "imperial consciousness" everywhere. According to political analyst Viktor Olevich, "It's a plan, a special operation, whatever you like to call it, but it's not just empty words."

Kazakhstani political analyst Rasul Zhumaly urges us not to ignore statements like these, but to respond to them promptly at state level: "Of course Russia is a large neighbour and has to be reckoned with, but it must play by the rules that are set out in bilateral documents and accepted in international relations, namely non-interference in domestic affairs and respect for each other's sovereignty and territorial integrity."

The border between Kazakhstan and Russia has long been on the agenda. In 1920 the Kazakh statesman and community leader Akhmet Baitursynov contributed to the debate. He made his position clear in a letter to Lenin dated 7 May 1920, in which he wrote that any change in the borders of the Kazakh Republic would be inadmissible.

And yet attempts are still being made to change our state borders. What, then, is the point of drawing up international treaties?

Every week Russia's Channel 1 broadcasts *The Great Game*, a programme that analyses current political events. The Russian point of view is presented by State Duma deputy and academic Vyacheslav Nikonov; the American perspective is given by Dmitri Simes, political scientist and chairman of the Center for the National Interest in the US. On the evening of 10 December

2020, as we were listening to the latest edition of *The Great Game*, Nikonov said live on air that "Kazakhstan just didn't exist… Basically, the territory of Kazakhstan is a big present from Russia and the Soviet Union."

My initial reaction on hearing this vacuous nonsense from Nikonov was utter outrage and apprehension. Goodness me, how generous of Russia to give us such a wonderful gift! How are we to understand such a provocative and insulting assertion?

The lines of a poem about Kazakhstan which I read out, loudly and with expression, on the main stage of the Palace of Culture as a small schoolgirl in the early 1970s, are firmly rooted in my memory:

"Look: Kazakhstan, shining and bright,
rises, clothed in a wonderful light.
From the Tien-Shan it stretches out wide
to the Urals all studded with jade.
The Kazakhs have a land of their own,
for ever and ever their home.
The Kazakhs, like a dream that's come true,
have their own law that's wise and fair too.
From the Kazakhs words flow like a stream
in their language so lively and free."

These lines are more relevant than ever today.

The Kazakh people has its own centuries-old history. Maybe some people are ignorant of it, but that doesn't mean it doesn't exist. It's up to everyone to educate themselves.

"…Kazakhstani senator Mukhtar Kul-Mukhammed gave a robust response to the Russian deputy's comments. He noted that Nikonov is the grandson of Vyacheslav Molotov, who signed a secret pact with Joachim von Ribbentrop two years before the Soviet Union entered the Second World War. Apparently he was also a Komsomol leader, ardent Communist Party organiser, and assistant to the controversial KGB chief Vadim Bakatin."

Does this kind of treachery run in the family? Nikonov needs to do some serious rereading of the history of Kazakhstan – not the history he has twisted to suit himself, but real, proper history. These are ancestral Kazakh lands in the full sense of the word. And no one has the right to unpick the seams of borders and sew them back again the way they want them. Russian political analysts have emphasised that in Russia "envy is everywhere present", and have hinted more than once that their rulers are always poking their noses into history, rewriting it, redrawing the map to suit them (Russian journalist and politician Alexander Khinshtein), and posting "a vast amount of lies on the Internet" (Russian political analyst Dmitry Nekrasov). Stalin, too, did a lot of redrawing of borders.

Nikonov was upfront in expressing his view about Russia's gift to Kazakhstan. But the big question is what remained unsaid. Everyone has their own demons. These undisclosed demons don't seem to have resulted in inevitable actions. Kazakhstan's Ministry of Foreign Affairs has noted that "certain Russian politicians' inflammatory attacks on Kazakhstan are seriously damaging to our relationship as allies".

Russian music producer Iosif Prigozhin was critical of Nikonov's sensationalist claim: "…All these people who come out with thoughtless remarks like these are polarising our society. This is highly dangerous… That's why we must build relationships carefully and tactfully, so as not to destroy what has taken many decades to create."

For his part, he called on society "to be wise and not jump to conclusions": "Right now, the most important thing is to nurture our relationships and not allow third parties to play us off against each other."

But how can insults like these be ignored? When children are playing they might not want to share; they quarrel, run off in different directions with their toys, then make up again. But these aren't little kids, but highly respected adults who knew exactly what they were saying. At least, they should always know what they're saying.

"Don't play along. The Soviet Union is no more. Moscow isn't the centre that decides the rules of the game."

Now to the question of returning seized land. Russia has annexed land in Moldova, Georgia and Ukraine without proper authorisation. The world is silent; no one can do anything against Russia, so they will continue to throw their weight around. They just can't get enough, they're not going to calm down, they'll go on expanding their territory, grabbing more and more. They make out that they're all sweetness and light, passing evil off as good, palming responsibility off onto others. So much remains hidden behind the scenes. Now they're angling for Kazakhstan. More mayhem, no honour, no principles. In Prigozhin's opinion, "They've already messed up Ukraine, they wanted to mess up Belarus, and now they want to stir things up in Kazakhstan … there's a feeling that we have subversive activities going on within Russia."

For me, the Soviet Union and everything associated with it was sacred. I remember how I felt when I joined the Pioneers and the Komsomol – I was trembling with unbelievable excitement. I was proud that I lived in a huge multi-ethnic country, I was proud to belong to it. I thought the members of these organisations were pure as the driven snow. I believed in justice, respected the feeling of responsibility, and tried my very best in whatever I did. I did not know that these organisations were full of deceit, dirt and decay. My epiphany came suddenly, like a bolt from the blue: the old certainties were destroyed, vanished, changed out of all recognition. The disappointment was hard to bear. What had previously seemed honest, reliable and structured, gradually fell apart. A feeling that something had been lost…

Sometimes I can't stop thinking about Russia's attitude towards Kazakhstan – it frightens me. Russia felt no pity for Ukraine. If that's how Russia treats a sister, fellow Slavs, what can Kazakhstan expect?

I am alarmed by the "attacks on Kazakhstan in some Russian media": "in the media and on TV, both journalists and guests insult and belittle others and, quite frankly, behave provocatively…"

When we were part of the Soviet Union, the Kazakhs were slaves. We grew up with shared slogans and no right to our own voice: one step out of line and you were shot. That slavery is over now. Put down the gun. Nothing lasts for ever; everything flows, everything changes. The old has been replaced with the new: we Kazakhs have our own land, inherited from our ancestors, our own country, our own government. All this is lawful and enshrined in the Constitution. We Kazakhs have definitely had enough of Russia telling us what to do. Let us breathe freely in our own country and be our own bosses.
"Kazakhstan should… be regarded as an ally, a strategic partner and a sovereign state, and the right of Kazakhstan and its people to deal with their own domestic problems should be respected." Kazakhstan is a free country, and in our own country we'll figure things out ourselves."

It isn't just in the former Soviet republics that Russia pursues a policy of inappropriate intervention and remodelling to its own taste. Russia "doesn't give a damn about other countries' national interests". Russia moves in on other countries' territory, pokes its nose into their domestic policies, turns everything inside out, brings everyone to heel, and loves to "impose its will on others". Everywhere it sets its own rules so that everything is nice and convenient for Russia, and does its best to "tighten economic control over its partners".
Maybe it's far more essential and more important to shift the focus to our own country, to put our own house in order and ensure prosperity so that our people don't sink into poverty? The Russian government is mired in deceit. It uses every means possible to whitewash itself, not just to its own people but to the rest of the world. "The hypocrisy of this government is off the scale." How long can this go on? Come to your senses, Russia, and cool your hotheads down! At the end of the day, you should be ashamed of yourself. I think you've done enough poking your nose into other countries' business and dragging your interests into those of other countries. Leave them all alone and look after your own country – a multi-ethnic federation – and all of its peoples. The time when you could dictate your own rules is past.

Russia gets involved in other countries' problems and makes already tense situations even tenser in order to distract its own citizens from the problems at home. It makes the situation in their country look better, paints a softer picture than in other (western) countries. This is a typically Russian knight's move – covering up the actual state of affairs so that the people don't panic. It requires a great deal of skill. After all, it matters how the information is presented, so to speak. In exercising its rights, the Russian government is buttering the people up. It knows just how to convince them, using nifty diversionary tactics and sophisticated methods. Maybe it should stop misusing them? Give your own citizens some peace and provide security and prosperity in your own country. Stop deceiving them and diverting their attention away from their immediate problems and onto the carve-up of territories and all these different political shows where they spout nonsense and have pointless discussions. Everyone on this earth wants peace and tranquillity, and sovereign states want to be separate and independent; they want to have friends, not enemies. To live in this world, we have to try to get on with each other and with our neighbours, not to cause harm, or wage clandestine wars, or play dirty games, or cross the line into inhumanity, but to build friendly and mutually beneficial relationships, and do good. Then the world will be a kinder, better, and more human place.

---

Russian fascism/chauvinism/Nazism has been with us for over a hundred years. All that changes is the leaders of the regime – the last of them being Lenin, Stalin and Putin. Putin the autocrat has mimicked Stalin, embraced his bloodthirsty forms of government, and assimilated his cruel, no-holds-barred methods in every way. There is plenty of proof of that, and plenty of shocking instances of dictatorship: the apartment buildings blown up near Moscow, the war in Chechnya, and in Syria, the bombing of the old town of Aleppo with its ancient world heritage. Putin has razed cities to the ground without a second thought and committed acts of barbarism on an extraordinary scale of brutality. So many totally innocent children and civilians have lost their lives... Instead of mourning, he has organised concerts; following his vicious atrocities, he forced the world to rebuild the city of Aleppo that he destroyed. There is nothing he will not stoop to; he has no qualms about playing dirty tricks; he runs roughshod over all that is sacred and inviolable. Human lives are worth nothing to him. This Russian fascist aggressor is trying to bring back the USSR and bring to heel all the nation-states that used to be part of it. And not just them. He's not going to stop here. His ultimate goal is to conquer Europe and Asia and establish a "Russian World". One single thought obsesses him: becoming the dictator of the whole world. He and all his embittered, zombified, Putin-worshipping accomplices think nothing of violating not just decisions, but even signed peace treaties on inviolability. Agreements signed with Russia aren't worth the paper they're printed on. To the Putin regime, no rules or values exist. The cynical individuals who do Putin's will – war criminals, scumbags, rapists – are selling their souls for money, glory and short-term gain. The aim of Putin's televisual propaganda is not to build up and develop his country, but to spread chauvinism, hypocrisy and aggression against democratic humanity. The TV presenters are degenerates who feed the masses with unbridled lies and turn them into idiots. Following their dictator's lead, they teach people to hate and steal and take things that don't belong to them. For Russians, fake news from the authorities is a familiar weapon of anti-human propaganda that the people soak up from their TV screens.

Russians are genetically different from other ethnic groups. They have elevated themselves to greatness with a megalomania that makes them incapable of any feeling: love, benevolence, sympathy, repentance, or compassion. Before, during and after 1941-1945, many ethnic groups were evacuated to Kazakhstan. To this day, they all express their gratitude to the Kazakhs for the help and support we offered. All of them. Except the Russians.

Despite Russia's impending demise, Russians continue to repeat the mantra of their greatness. They will be held to account for everything they have done; they will pay the price. The

Ukrainians are heroically risking their lives to defend their freedom, their children and their territory from the marauders and occupiers, and they are defending the whole world against Putin's vileness and brutality. I believe that Ukraine will soon be victorious in this war that has been going on since 2014. That victory will mean a victory for democracy and truth, a victory for all that is holy, good and human over the evil, animosity and hatred of Putin's fascism.

The Ukrainian people are a clear example of the right path to democracy. I am grateful to the US, UK, Turkey, Poland, the Czech Republic, the Baltic states, Canada, Japan, Australia and all the other countries that are helping Ukraine. Unfortunately, I do not understand the watch-and-wait stance that some major European nations (Italy, France, Germany, Austria, Hungary and Serbia) are taking. It looks as if in their hearts, they are on the side of Ruscism. The astronomical billions in hand-outs they receive from Putin are more important to them. I hope there will be a purge of corrupt and crooked countries from NATO following Ukraine's victory so that it no longer contains any treacherous, doubting and ambivalent member-states.

Almighty One, save and protect us from the universal establishment of the "Russian World"! May each people live peacefully according to its own ways, culture, traditions and customs, and with its peace on its territories.

---

I had long cherished the desire to publish this book of reminiscences and to gather my notes together, because written records fade away and don't keep for long. I felt the need to share these reminiscences with you, my dear reader, because they contain so much that is shared by and relevant to our whole country and our people, and they ought to be known to everyone. I kept putting it off until later, and "later" never happened. I set out my notes in the form they are in now in 2015. However, for very good reasons, they were not published at that time. I reviewed what I had written and added more. If you are reading these lines now, it means I have finally succeeded.
Thank you to all my readers.

I confess that I should like this book to be translated into many other languages of the peoples of the world; for there to be no tragedies, wars, grief or misery in any corner of planet Earth; for people everywhere to live in peace, health and friendship, respect and harmony, kindness and joy, prosperity and wellbeing, without trickery or deceit, long and happily, surrounded by love, warmth, care and support from family and friends; for babies to be born healthy, and life on Earth to continue.
Wishing you all good health, success and happiness all the days of your lives.

---

Yours, with heartfelt warmest wishes,
Lyalya Umirzakova

Contact details:
e-mail: L.Umirzakova@gmail.com

---

## BIBLIOGRAPHY

Razumov, Ilya. *The Dating of Nostradamus' Quatrains and Watercolours from the 'Lost Book'*. Ilya Razumov and Vladimir Petrov, Kyiv, Strelbitsky Multimedia Publishing, 2016. 670 pp. URL: https://litres.ru/ E-book.

Belger, Herold. *The Kazakh Word*. Herold Belger, Kazakhstan, 2001. 40 pp. URL: https://lit.kz/ E-book.

Information from the following websites was also used:

the Kazakh Service of the international media company Radio Azattyq, https://azattyq.org,
Kazakhstan's main news portal, https://tengrinews.kz
the news site https://ru.sputnik.kz,
https://vernoye-almaty.kz/aport.shtml,
https://caa-network.org,
https://wikipedia.org
and TV shows on politics.

## ABOUT THE AUTHOR

In this book, Lyalya Umirzakova shares true stories about one of the most infamous, cruel and ruthless figures of the 20th century.

Drawing on reminiscences that have long been preserved by an intimate circle of close family members, Lyalya tells of the years of terror, of crimes against humanity and lives destroyed, accompanying these notes with her own reflections and comments.

This book is intended for a wide range of readers.

www.ingramcontent.com/pod-product-compliance
Lightning Source LLC
LaVergne TN
LVHW020608200726
843509LV00001B/21